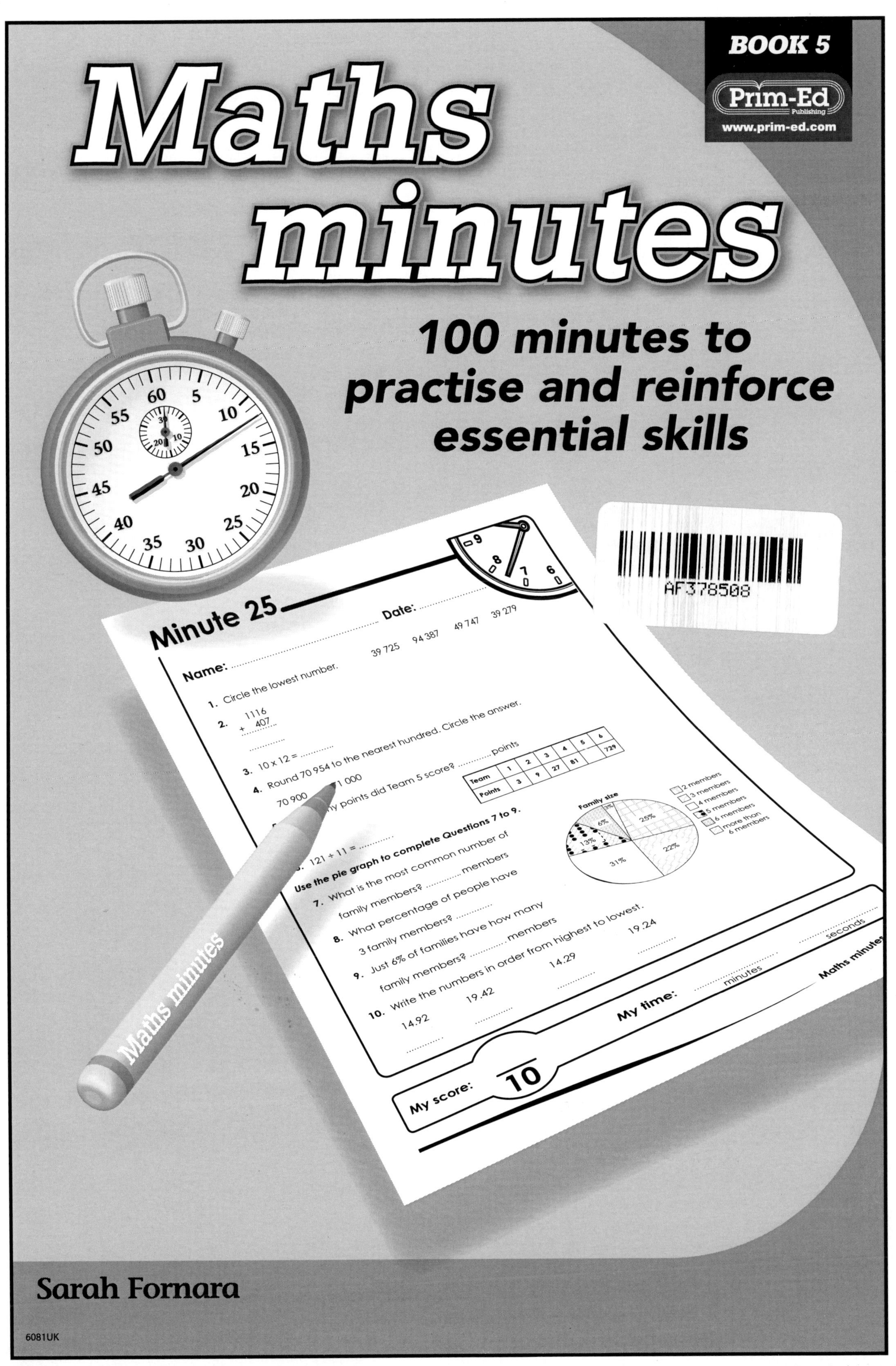

BOOK 5
Prim-Ed
Publishing
www.prim-ed.com
Maths minutes
100 minutes to practise and reinforce essential skills
Sarah Fornara
AF378508
6081UK

Maths minutes *Book 5*

Published by Prim-Ed Publishing® 2011 under licence to
Creative Teaching Press.
Copyright© 2005 Creative Teaching Press.
This version copyright© Prim-Ed Publishing® 2011

ISBN 978-1-84654-292-3
PR–6081

Titles available in this series:

Maths minutes – Book 1 *(Ages 5–6)*
Maths minutes – Book 2 *(Ages 6–7)*
Maths minutes – Book 3 *(Ages 7–8)*
Maths minutes – Book 4 *(Ages 8–9)*
Maths minutes – Book 5 *(Ages 9–10)*
Maths minutes – Book 6 *(Ages 10–11)*

Internet websites
In some cases, websites or specific URLs may be recommended. While these are checked and rechecked at the time of publication,
the publisher has no control over any subsequent changes which may be made to webpages. It is *strongly* recommended that the class
teacher checks *all* URLs before allowing pupils to access them.

View all pages online

Website: www.prim-ed.com

MATHS MINUTES – BOOK 5

Foreword

Maths minutes is a six-book series for pupils in primary schools, that provides a structured daily programme of easy-to-follow activities in the mathematics areas of: **number, algebra, shape and space, measurement** and **handling data.**

The programme provides a framework to:

* *promote the ongoing learning of essential maths concepts and skills through practice and reinforcement*
* *develop and maintain speed of recall and maths fluency*
* *develop knowledge and understanding of mathematics terminology*
* *encourage mental maths strategies*
* *provide support to the overall daily mathematics programme.*

Maths minutes – Book 5 features 100 'minutes', each with 10 classroom-tested problems. The problems provide the pupils with practice in the key areas of mathematics for their year level, and basic computational skills. Designed to be implemented in numerical order from 1 to 100, the activities in *Maths minutes* are developmental through each book and across the series.

Comprehensive teachers notes, record-keeping charts, a scope-and-sequence table (showing when each new concept and skill is introduced), and photocopiable pupil reference materials are also included.

How many minutes does it take to complete a 'maths minute'?

Pupils will enjoy challenging themselves as they apply their mathematical knowledge and understanding to complete a 'maths minute' in the fastest possible time.

Titles available in this series:	**Age levels**
• Maths minutes – *Book 1*	Age 5–6 years
• Maths minutes – *Book 2*	Age 6–7 years
• Maths minutes – *Book 3*	Age 7–8 years
• Maths minutes – *Book 4*	Age 8–9 years
• Maths minutes – *Book 5*	Age 9–10 years
• Maths minutes – *Book 6*	Age 10–11 years

Contents

Teachers notes

How to use this book

Maths minutes can be used in a variety of ways, such as:

- **a speed test**. As the teacher starts a stopwatch, pupils begin the 'minute'. As each pupil finishes, he/she raises a hand and the teacher calls out the time. The pupil records this time on the appropriate place on the sheet. Alternatively, a particular time can be allocated for the whole class to complete the 'minute' in. Pupils record their scores and time on their 'minute journal' (see page vii).
- **a whole-class activity**. Work through the 'minute' together as a teaching or reviewing activity.
- **a warm-up activity**. Use a 'minute' a day as a 'starter' or warm-up activity before the main part of the maths lesson begins.
- **a homework activity**. If given as a homework activity, it would be most beneficial for the pupils if the 'minute' is corrected and reviewed at the start of the following lesson.

Maths minutes strategies

Encourage pupils to apply the following strategies to help improve their scores and decrease the time taken to complete the 10 questions.

- To use mental maths strategies whenever possible.
- To move quickly down the page, answering the problems they know first.
- To come back to problems they are unsure of, after they have completed all other problems.
- To make educated guesses when they encounter problems they are not familiar with.
- To rewrite word problems as number problems.

A *Maths minute* pupil activity page.

Name and date
Pupils write their name and the date in the spaces provided.

Questions
There are 10 problems, providing practice in every key area of the maths strands.

Score
Pupils record their score out of 10 in the space provided.

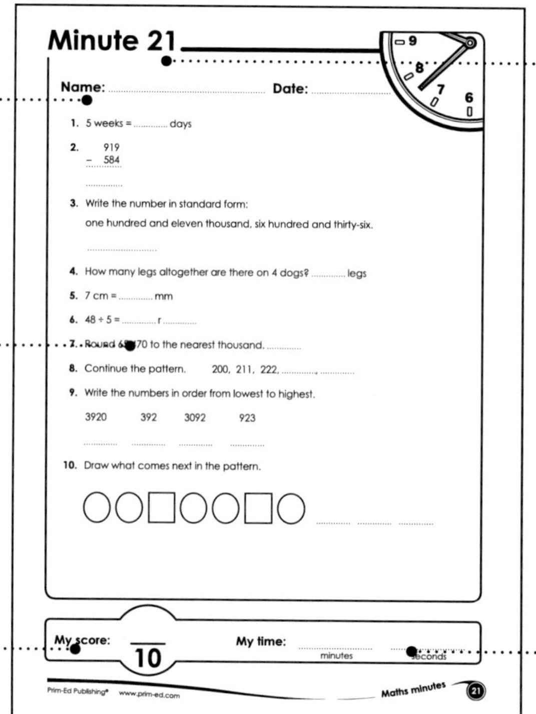

'Maths minute' number
Maths minutes are designed to be completed in numerical order.

Time
Pupils record the time taken to complete the 'minute' at the bottom of the sheet. (This is optional.)

Teachers notes

Marking

Answers are provided for all activities. How these activities are marked will vary according to the teacher's organisational policy. Methods could include whole-class checking, partner checking, individual pupil checking, or collection by the teacher.

Diagnosis of problem areas

Maths minutes provides the teacher with immediate feedback of whole-class and individual pupil understanding. This information is useful for future programming and planning of further opportunities to practise and review the skills and concepts which need addressing.

Make use of the structured nature of the questions to diagnose problem areas; rather than asking who got 10 out of 10, ask the pupils who got Number 1 correct to raise their hands, Number 2, Number 3 etc. This way you will be able to quickly determine which concepts and calculations are causing problems for the majority of the pupils. Once the routine of *Maths minutes* is established, the teacher will have time to work with individuals or small groups to assist them with any areas causing problems.

Meeting the needs of individuals

The structure of *Maths minutes* allows some latitude in the way the books are used; for example, it may be impractical (as well as demoralising for some) for all pupils to be using the same book. It can also be difficult for teachers to manage the range of abilities found in any one classroom, so while pupils may be working at different levels from different books, the familiar structure makes it easier to cope with individual differences. An outline of the suggested age range levels each book is suited to is given on page iii.

Additional resources:

- **Minute records**

  Teachers can record pupil scores and times on the **Minute records** table located on page vi.

- **Scope and sequence**

  The **Scope-and-sequence table** gives the 'minute' in which each new skill and concept appears for the first time.

- **Minute journal**

  Once a 'minute' is completed, pupils record their score and time on their **Minute journal**, located on page vii.

- **Useful maths facts**

  Three pages of photocopiable pupil reference materials have been included, which pupils can refer to when required.

- **Answers to all questions are found on pages 101 to 105.**

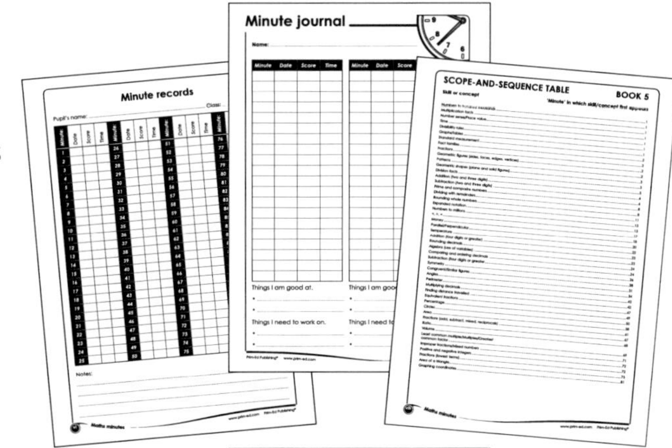

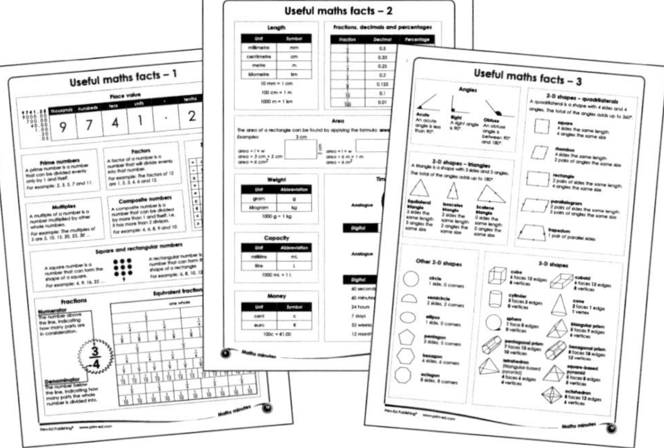

Maths minutes

Minute records

Pupil's name: .... Class: ....

Minute:	Date	Score	Time	Minute:	Date	Score	Time	Minute:	Date	Score	Time	Minute:	Date	Score	Time
1				26				51				76			
2				27				52				77			
3				28				53				78			
4				29				54				79			
5				30				55				80			
6				31				56				81			
7				32				57				82			
8				33				58				83			
9				34				59				84			
10				35				60				85			
11				36				61				86			
12				37				62				87			
13				38				63				88			
14				39				64				89			
15				40				65				90			
16				41				66				91			
17				42				67				92			
18				43				68				93			
19				44				69				94			
20				45				70				95			
21				46				71				96			
22				47				72				97			
23				48				73				98			
24				49				74				99			
25				50				75				100			

Notes:

....

....

....

....

Maths minutes

Minute journal

Name: ....

Minute	Date	Score	Time

Minute	Date	Score	Time

Things I am good at.

• ....

• ....

Things I need to work on.

• ....

• ....

Things I am good at.

• ....

• ....

Things I need to work on.

• ....

• ....

SCOPE-AND-SEQUENCE TABLE

BOOK 5

Skill or concept	'Minute' in which skill/concept first appears

Maths minutes

Useful maths facts – 1

Place value

	thousands	hundreds	tens	units	•	tenths	hundredths
9 7 4 1 . 2 5 9000.00 700.00 40.00 1.00 .20 .05	9	7	4	1	•	2	5

Prime numbers

A prime number is a number that can be divided evenly only by 1 and itself.

For example: 2, 3, 5, 7 and 11.

Multiples

A multiple of a number is a number multiplied by other whole numbers.

For example: The multiples of 5 are 5, 10, 15, 20, 25, 30 …

Factors

A factor of a number is a number that will divide evenly into that number.

For example: The factors of 12 are 1, 2, 3, 4, 6 and 12.

Composite numbers

A composite number is a number that can be divided by more than 1 and itself; i.e. it has more than 2 divisors.

For example: 4, 6, 8, 9 and 10.

Symbols

+	addition
–	subtraction
x	multiplication
÷	division
=	equal to
p	pence
£	pound
<	less than
>	greater than

Square and rectangular numbers

A square number is a number that can form the shape of a square.

For example: 4, 9, 16, 25 …

9

A rectangular number is a number that can form the shape of a rectangle.

For example: 6, 8, 10, 12 …

6

Fractions

Numerator

The number above the line, indicating how many parts are in consideration.

$$\frac{3}{4}$$

Denominator

The number below the line, indicating how many parts the whole number is divided into.

Equivalent fractions

one whole											
$\frac{1}{2}$						$\frac{1}{2}$					
$\frac{1}{4}$			$\frac{1}{4}$			$\frac{1}{4}$			$\frac{1}{4}$		
$\frac{1}{8}$		$\frac{1}{8}$		$\frac{1}{8}$		$\frac{1}{8}$		$\frac{1}{8}$		$\frac{1}{8}$	$\frac{1}{8}$ $\frac{1}{8}$
$\frac{1}{3}$				$\frac{1}{3}$				$\frac{1}{3}$			
$\frac{1}{6}$		$\frac{1}{6}$		$\frac{1}{6}$		$\frac{1}{6}$		$\frac{1}{6}$		$\frac{1}{6}$	
$\frac{1}{9}$	$\frac{1}{9}$	$\frac{1}{9}$	$\frac{1}{9}$	$\frac{1}{9}$	$\frac{1}{9}$	$\frac{1}{9}$	$\frac{1}{9}$	$\frac{1}{9}$			
$\frac{1}{12}$	$\frac{1}{12}$	$\frac{1}{12}$	$\frac{1}{12}$	$\frac{1}{12}$	$\frac{1}{12}$	$\frac{1}{12}$	$\frac{1}{12}$	$\frac{1}{12}$	$\frac{1}{12}$	$\frac{1}{12}$	$\frac{1}{12}$
$\frac{1}{5}$		$\frac{1}{5}$		$\frac{1}{5}$		$\frac{1}{5}$		$\frac{1}{5}$			
$\frac{1}{10}$	$\frac{1}{10}$	$\frac{1}{10}$	$\frac{1}{10}$	$\frac{1}{10}$	$\frac{1}{10}$	$\frac{1}{10}$	$\frac{1}{10}$	$\frac{1}{10}$	$\frac{1}{10}$		

Useful maths facts – 2

Length

Unit	Symbol
millimetre	mm
centimetre	cm
metre	m
kilometre	km

10 mm = 1 cm

100 cm = 1 m

1000 m = 1 km

Fractions, decimals and percentages

Fraction	Decimal	Percentage
$\frac{1}{2}$	0.5	50%
$\frac{1}{3}$	0.33	33%
$\frac{1}{4}$	0.25	25%
$\frac{1}{5}$	0.2	20%
$\frac{1}{8}$	0.125	12.5%
$\frac{1}{10}$	0.1	10%
$\frac{1}{100}$	0.01	1%

Area

The area of a rectangle can be found by applying the formula: **area = length × width**

Examples:

area = l × w
area = 3 cm × 2 cm
area = 6 cm^2

area = l × w
area = 6 m × 1 m
area = 6 m^2

Weight

Unit	Abbreviation
gram	g
kilogram	kg

1000 g = 1 kg

Capacity

Unit	Abbreviation
millilitre	mL
litre	L

1000 mL = 1 L

Money

Unit	Symbol
pence	p
pound	£

100p = £1.00

Time

Analogue

Digital	7.15

Analogue

Digital	1.50

60 seconds	=	1 minute
60 minutes	=	1 hour
24 hours	=	1 day
7 days	=	1 week
52 weeks	=	1 year
12 months	=	1 year

Useful maths facts – 3

Angles

 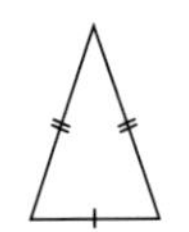 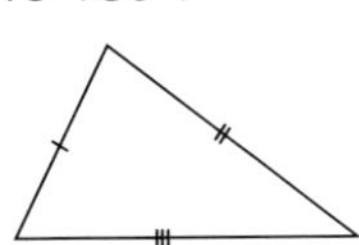

Acute
An acute angle is less than 90°.

Right
A right angle is 90°.

Obtuse
An obtuse angle is between 90° and 180°.

2-D shapes – triangles

A triangle is a shape with 3 sides and 3 angles. The total of the angles adds up to 180°.

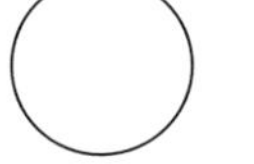  

Equilateral triangle
3 sides the same length
3 angles the same size

Isosceles triangle
2 sides the same length
2 angles the same size

Scalene triangle
0 sides the same length
0 angles the same size

2-D shapes – quadrilaterals

A quadrilateral is a shape with 4 sides and 4 angles. The total of the angles adds up to 360°.

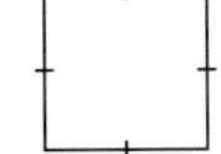
square
4 sides the same length
4 angles the same size

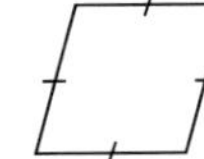
rhombus
4 sides the same length
2 pairs of angles the same size

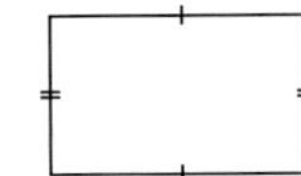
rectangle
2 pairs of sides the same length
4 angles the same size

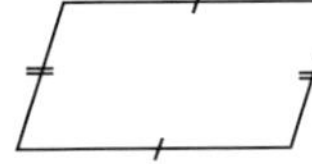
parallelogram
2 pairs of sides the same length
2 pairs of angles the same size

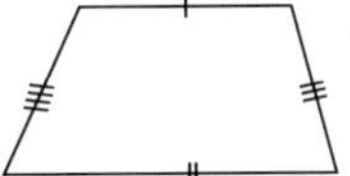
trapezium
1 pair of parallel sides

Other 2-D shapes

circle
1 side, 0 corners

semicircle
2 sides, 2 corners

ellipse
1 side, 0 corners

pentagon
5 sides, 5 corners

hexagon
6 sides, 6 corners

octagon
8 sides, 8 corners

3-D shapes

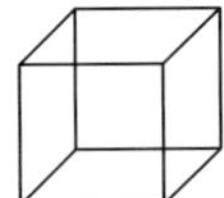
cube
6 faces **12** edges
8 vertices

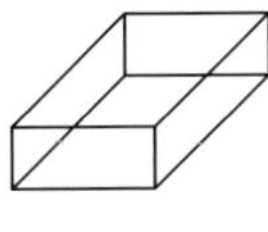
cuboid
6 faces **12** edges
8 vertices

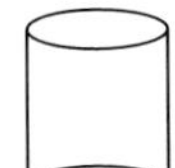
cylinder
3 faces **2** edges
0 vertices

cone
2 faces **1** edge
1 vertex

sphere
1 face **0** edges
0 vertices

triangular prism
5 faces **9** edges
6 vertices

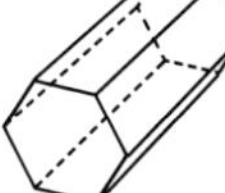
pentagonal prism
7 faces **15** edges
10 vertices

hexagonal prism
8 faces **18** edges
12 vertices

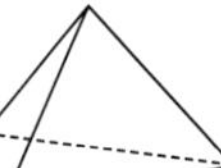
tetrahedron
(triangular-based pyramid)
4 faces **6** edges
4 vertices

square-based pyramid
5 faces **8** edges
5 vertices

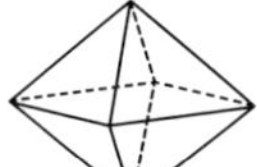
octahedron
8 faces **12** edges
6 vertices

  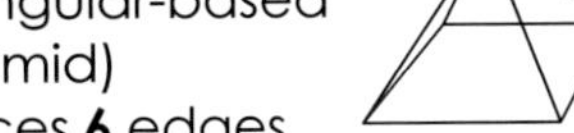

Notes

Minute 1

Name: .... **Date:** ....

1. For 902 798, write the digit in the hundreds place. ....

2. 6 x 2 = ...

3. Can 351 be evenly divided by 2? Circle: Yes or No

4. 80 ÷ 8 = ...

5. Write the time 3 hours after 9.00 pm. ....

Use the pie chart to complete Questions 6 to 8.

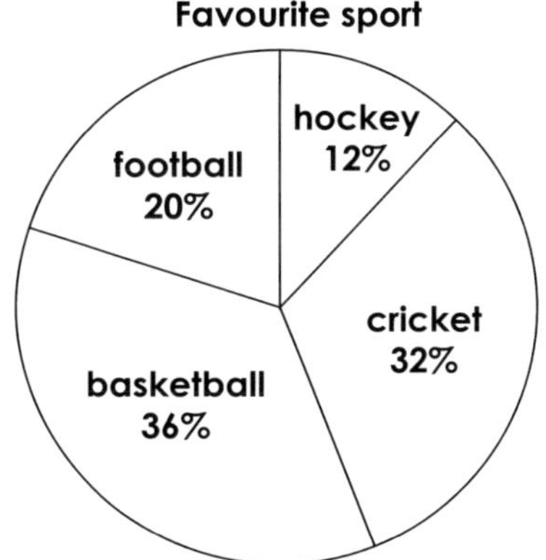

6. What percentage of people

   prefer cricket? ....

7. What two sports together equal the same

   percentage as cricket? .... and

   ....

8. Which sport has the greatest percentage? ....

9. How many sides does a rectangle have? .... sides

10. 1 metre = ... centimetres

My score: ______ / **10**

My time: ....
minutes   seconds

Minute 2

Name: .... **Date:** ....

Use the pictogram to complete Questions 1 to 3.

1. How many books did Eva read? .... books

2. How many more books did Eva read than Diana? .... books

3. Two pupils read the minimum number of books. How many books did they each read? .... books

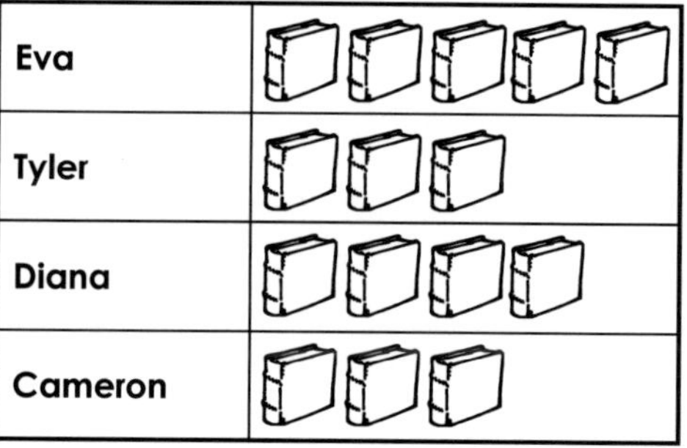

4. 77 ÷ 7 = ...

5. How many sides does a **pentagon** have? .... sides

6. Write the missing family fact.

   14 − 8 = 6   14 − 6 = 8

   6 + 8 = 14   8 + □ = □

7. The value of the bold digit in **3**26 619 is three hundred thousand.

   Circle: True   or   False

8. Write a fraction for the shaded area. .... 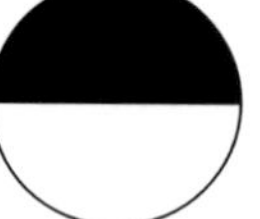

9. 1 minute = ... seconds

10. Continue the pattern.

    0, 3, 6, 9, ..., ..., ...

My score: ——— / **10**

My time: .... minutes   .... seconds

Minute 3

Name: .... **Date:** ....

1. Write this number in standard form:

   four hundred and seventy-three thousand, six hundred and sixty-five.

   ....

2. 80 ÷ 10 = ...

Use the pie chart to complete Questions 3 to 5.

3. What do the lowest percentage of children do

   on Saturday? ....

4. What do 35% of the

   children do? ....

5. Do more children play outside

   or watch a film? ....

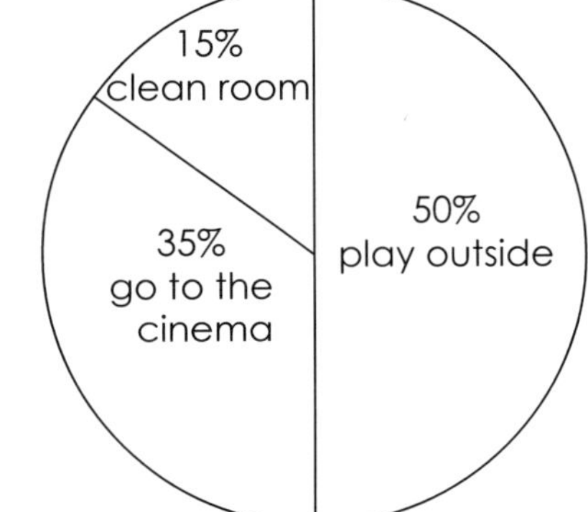

6. 7 x 7 = ...

7. What time is 14 hours after 3.00 am? ....

8. Circle the name of the solid shape.   sphere   cone   cylinder   pyramid

9. Complete the equation for 'The difference between 8 and 12 equals 4'.

   [ ] − [ ] = [ ]

10. Double 70. ....

My score: ______
10

My time: ....
                          minutes   seconds

Minute 4

Name: .... **Date:** ....

Use the bar graph to complete Questions 1 to 3.

1. How many tins did Mrs Berry's

   class collect? .... tins

2. How many tins did Mr Phelps'

   class collect? .... tins

3. What was the total number of

   tins collected? .... tins

4. Write the missing family fact.

   $42 \div 7 = 6$

   $42 \div 6 = 7$

   $7 \times 6 = 42$

   $6 \times \boxed{} = \boxed{}$

5. 4 years = ... months

6. 1 cm = ... mm

7. $80 \div 4 =$ ....

8. Write a fraction for the number of shaded triangles. ....

   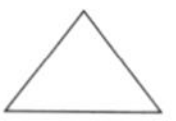

9. $6 \times 8 =$ ....

10. Circle the rule for the sequence: 98, 87, 76, 65.

    Add 10   Subtract 10   Add 11   Subtract 11

My score: $\dfrac{}{10}$ **My time:** ....
                                                    minutes   seconds

Minute 5

Name: .... **Date:** ....

1. $100 \div 20 =$ ....

2. $10 \times 4 =$ ....

3. 1 km = 1000 m

   18 km = ... m

4. Can 917 be evenly divided by 5?   Circle: Yes   or   No

5.   47
     +   22
     ....

     ....

6. Circle the greatest number.

   87 987   646 354   305 003

7. Write a fraction for the number of shaded squares. ....

8. Continue the pattern.

   72, 62, 52, ..., ..., ...

Use the table to complete Question 9 and 10.

Price	£2	£4	£6	£8	£10
Number of raffle tickets	5	10	15		

9. How many tickets would £8 buy? .... tickets

10. How many tickets would £10 buy? .... tickets

My score: $\dfrac{}{10}$ **My time:** ....
                 minutes   seconds

Minute 6

Name: .... **Date:** ....

1. $8 + 8 + 5 =$ ....

2.
$$\begin{array}{r} 497 \\ -253 \\ \hline \end{array}$$
....

3. Complete the equation for 'the sum of six and seven'. $\square + \square = \square$

4. $8 \times 10 =$ ....

5. $21 \div 3 =$ ....

6. 1 kg = ... g

7. 2, 3, 5, 7, 11 are all prime numbers.　Circle:　True　or　False

8. How many centimetres are in 2 metres? .... centimetres

9. $65 \div 5 =$ ....

10. Circle the name of the solid shape.

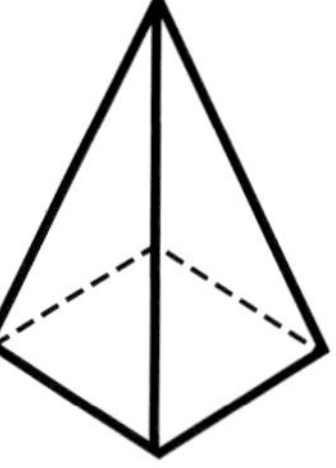

square pyramid　　　　rectangular pyramid　　　　triangular pyramid

My score: $\dfrac{}{10}$　　　**My time:** ....
minutes　　　　seconds

Minute 7

Name: .... **Date:** ....

1. Write the missing family fact.

    $3 + 8 = 11$ $8 + 3 = 11$ $11 - 8 = 3$

    ☐ – ☐ = ☐

2. $\begin{array}{r} 267 \\ +\ \ 32 \\ \hline \end{array}$

Use the line graph to complete Questions 3 and 4.

3. How many days of perfect attendance were there in March? .... days

4. Did the perfect attendance **increase** or **decrease** from April to May? ....

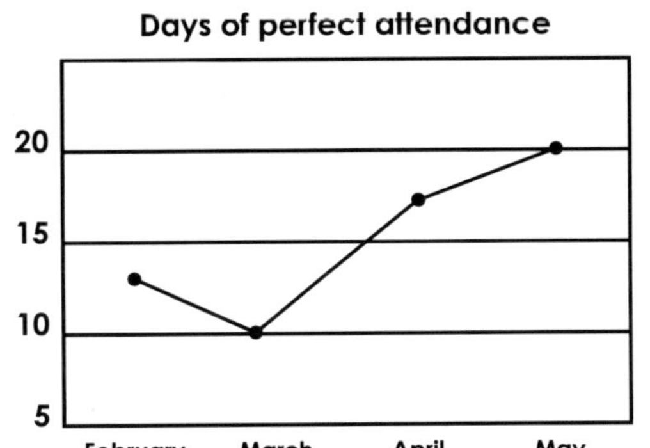

Days of perfect attendance

5. $4 \times 6 =$ ....

6. 1 cm = ... mm

7. 1 km = 1000 m

    1.5 km = ... m

8. 120, 110, 100, ..., ..., ...

9. Write a fraction for the number of shaded stars. ....

    ★ ☆ ★ ☆ ☆ ★ ☆

10. $4\overline{)800}$

My score: $\dfrac{}{10}$

My time: ....
minutes   seconds

Minute 8

Name: .... **Date:** ....

1. Round 684 to the nearest hundred. ....

2.   107
     + 314
     ....

     ....

3. Write an equation for 'the product of 12 and 8'.

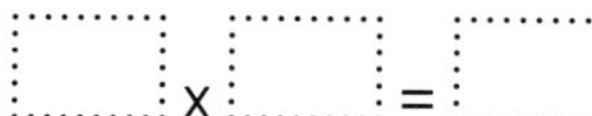

4. 7 x 8 = ...

5. A prime number is a whole number greater than 1 that has only itself

   and 1 as factors.   Circle: True   or   False

6. Write the time 11 hours after 5.00 pm. ....

7. $8\overline{)64}$

8. Write the name of the shape. ....

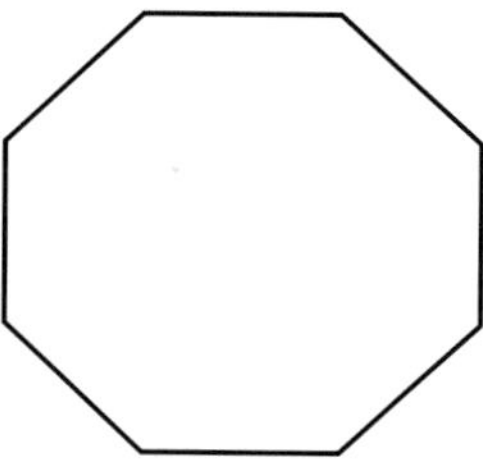

9. 1 kg = 1000 g   3 kilograms = ... grams

10. Circle the answer for $2\overline{)203}$.

    10 r 3   101 r 3   101 r 1

My score: ______
10

My time: ....
                    minutes   seconds

Minute 9

Name: .... **Date:** ....

1. For 902 798, write the digit in the ten thousands place. ....

2. Circle the answer for 32 + 54.   66   76   86

Use the pie chart to complete Questions 3 and 4.

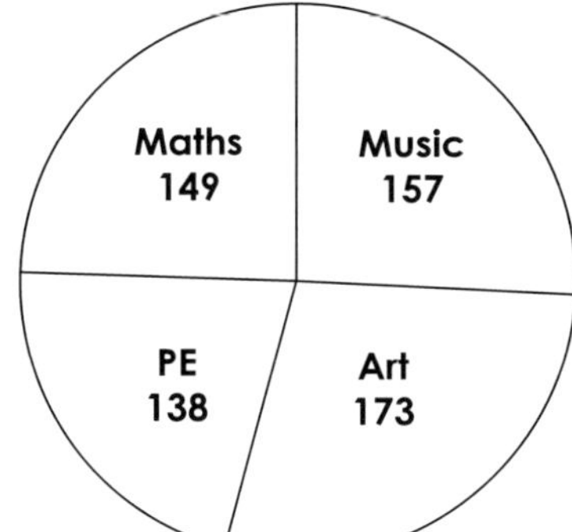

3. How many pupils like music

   the best? .... pupils

4. Which subject is liked the least? ....

5. 10 x 6 = ...

6. 45 ÷ 5 = ...

7. 1 L = ... mL

8. Write a fraction for the number of shaded cans. ....

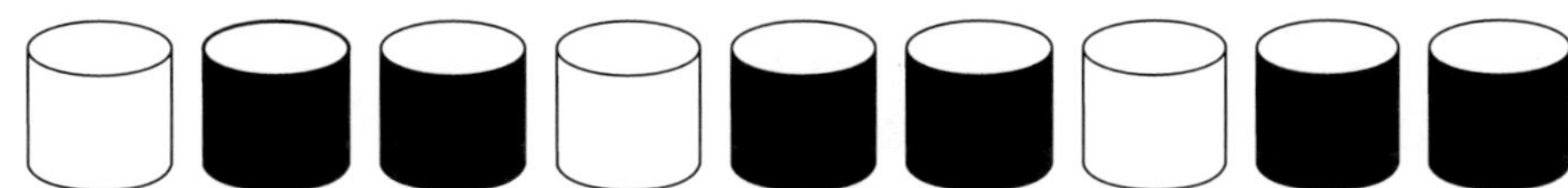

9. Write the measurement as shown by the arrow. .... centimetres

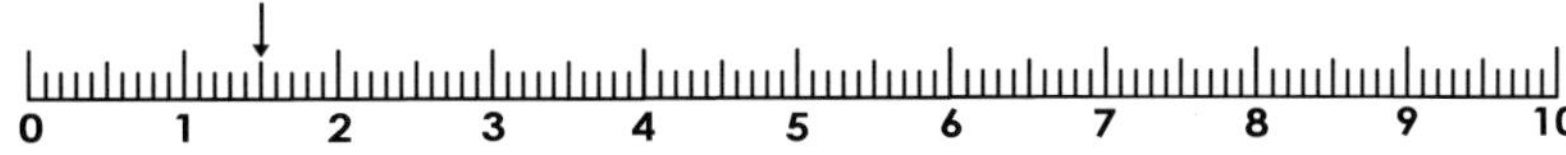

10. How many sides does a **hexagon** have? .... sides

My score: ______
10

My time: ....
                    minutes   seconds

Minute 10

Name: .... **Date:** ....

1. Name the value of the bold digit. 101 **7**00 ....

2. Round 1064 to the nearest thousand. ....

3. 6 x 6 = ...

4. Can 192 be evenly divided by 3?   Circle: Yes   or   No

5. Write a fraction for the shaded area. ....

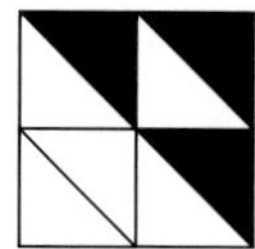

6. 70 + 80 = ...

7. Complete the equation for 'the product of 7 and 11'.   7 [   ] 11 = [   ]

8. (8 + 3) + 6 = ...

Use the table to complete Questions 9 and 10.

Reading challenge

Books read	25	50	75
Free pizzas	1	2	3

9. How many free pizzas would you get if you read 100 books? .... pizzas

10. How many books would you have to read if you wanted 6 free pizzas?

    .... books

My score: $\dfrac{\quad}{10}$ **My time:** ....
                              minutes   seconds

Minute 11

Name: .... **Date:** ....

1. 800 000 + 30 000 + 1000 + 800 + 90 + 4 = ...

2. 10 x 5 = ...

3.
$$\begin{array}{r} 993 \\ -\quad 85 \\ \hline \end{array}$$
   ....

4. Is 29 a prime number?   Circle: Yes   or   No

5. 36 ÷ 6 = ...

6. 15 cm = ... mm

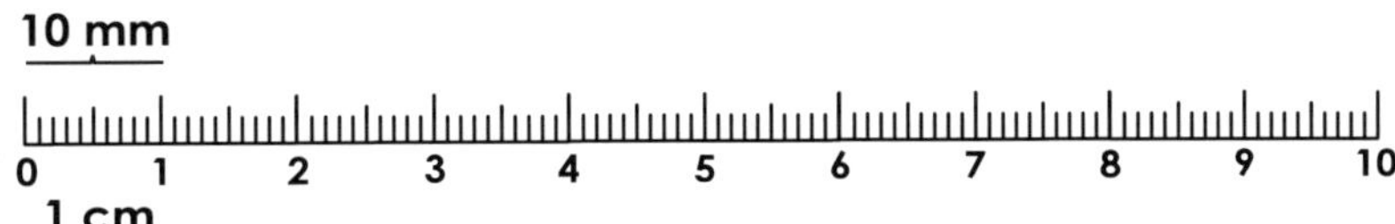

7. (7 + 5) + 9 = ...

8. Complete the equation for 'the difference between 86 and 42'.

   86 [......] 42 = [......]

9. Write the name of the figure. ....

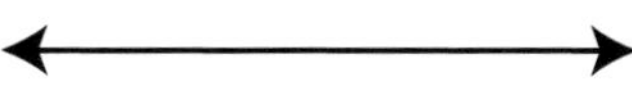

10. 1 kg = 1000 g

    15 kg = ... g

My score: ______
     10

My time: ....
                     minutes   seconds

Minute 12

Name: .... **Date:** ....

1.   819
     − 275

     ....

2. Continue the pattern.   20, 24, 28, ..., ..., ...

3. $3\overline{)42}$

4. 1 cm = 10 mm   68 cm = ... mm

5. Write the number in standard form:

   nine hundred and thirty-three thousand and eighty-five. ....

6. Write the time 23 hours after 8.00 pm. ....

7. Write the missing family fact.

   $4 \times 7 = 28$

   $7 \times 4 = 28$

   $28 \div 4 = 7$

   ☐ ÷ ☐ = ☐

Use the pie chart to complete Questions 8 and 9.

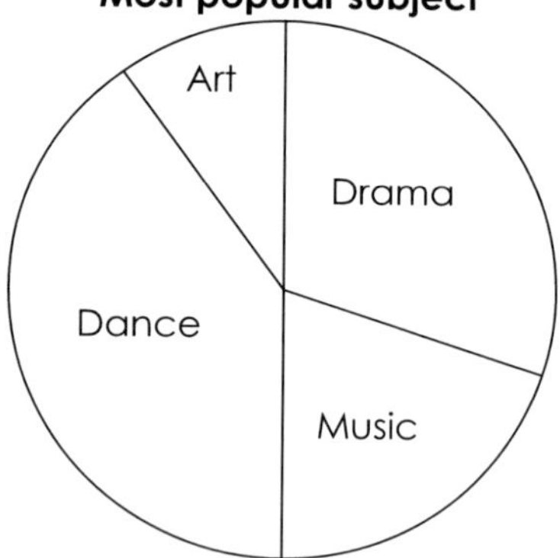

8. Which subject do most pupils

   enjoy? ....

9. Which subject is more popular: Drama or Music? ....

10. Write the name of the solid shape. .... 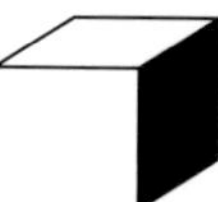

My score: $\dfrac{}{10}$ **My time:** ....

                                         minutes   seconds

Minute 13

Name: .... **Date:** ....

1. In 7 582 206, the digit 7 is in what place? ....

Use the pictogram to complete Questions 2 and 3.

2. How many angelfish are there?

   .... angelfish

3. How many more goldfish are there

   than tetras? .... more goldfish

4. Use <, > or =.

   512 [......] 521

5. 12 x 3 = ...

6. Can 504 be evenly divided by 6?   Circle: Yes or No

7. 1L = 1000 mL   3L = ... mL

8.   7902
   + 708
   ....

   ....

9. Write the fraction for the shaded area. ....

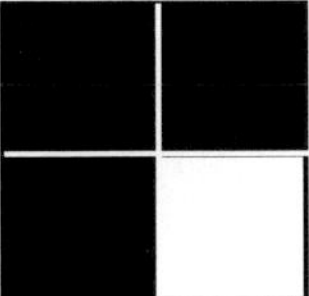

10. 7)‾10   r ....

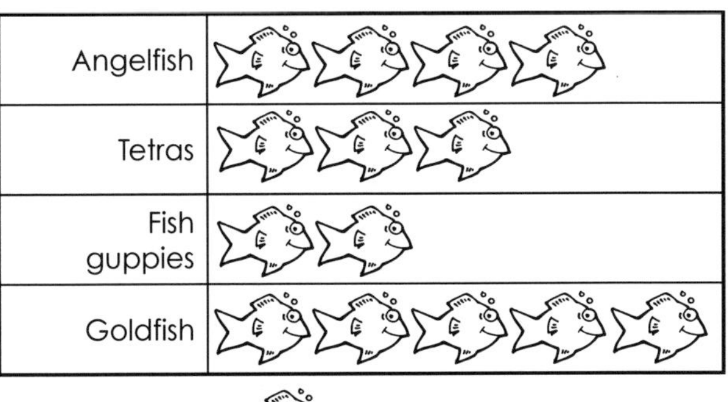

Fred's fish shop

Angelfish	🐟🐟🐟🐟
Tetras	🐟🐟🐟
Fish guppies	🐟🐟
Goldfish	🐟🐟🐟🐟🐟

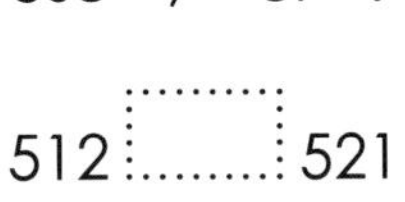 **equals 5 fish**

My score: _____ **10**

My time: ....
minutes   seconds

Minute 14

Name: .... **Date:** ....

1. 17 + 3 + 8 = ...

2. The **product** of 3 and 6 is ....

3.   643
   −   108
   ....

   ....

4. Is 54 a prime number or a composite number? ....

5.   5
        3
   +   7
   ....

   ....

6. Write the measurement as shown by the arrow. .... centimetres.

7. Continue the pattern.   1, 3, 5, ..., ..., ...

8. One decade = ... years

9. Write 42 234 in words. ....

   ....

10. Write the name of the solid shape. ....

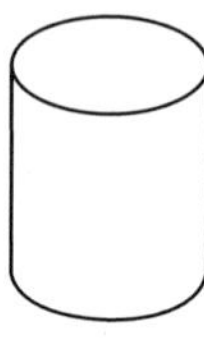

My score: _______   **My time:** ....

10   minutes   seconds

Minute 15

Name: .... **Date:** ....

1. Round 6705 to the nearest thousand. ....

2. Circle the digit in the **tenths** place. 742.943

3. 50 divided by 5 equals ....

4.
$$\begin{array}{r} 9809 \\ -\ \ 818 \\ \hline \\ \end{array}$$

5. 1 m = ... mm

6. Use < or >.   46 702 .... 46 802

7.
$$\begin{array}{r} 4 \\ 2 \\ 5 \\ +\ \ 8 \\ \hline \\ \end{array}$$

8. Write the name of the solid shape. ....

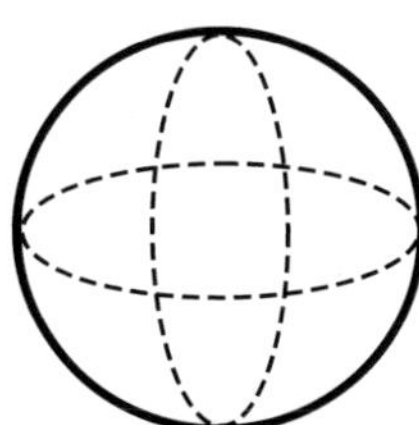

9. Continue the pattern.   2, 4, 8, 16, ..., ..., ...

10. Double 700. ....

My score: $\dfrac{}{10}$ **My time:** ....
                                                              minutes   seconds

Minute 16

Name: .... **Date:** ....

1. Use <, > or =.   641 967 [   ] 641 897

2. Round 94 385 to the nearest hundred. ....

3. 10 x 7 = ...

4. A composite number has more than two factors.   Circle: True   or   False

5. Continue the pattern.   21, 28, 35, ..., ..., ...

6. Write the missing family fact.

   3 x 8 = 24

   24 ÷ 8 = 3

   24 ÷ 3 = 8

   [   ] x [   ] = [   ]

Use the table to complete Questions 7 and 8.

Mealworms	20	40	60
Lizards	1	2	3

7. How many mealworms would be needed to feed 4 lizards?

   .... mealworms

8. How many lizards could you feed with 100 mealworms? .... lizards

9. Circle the digit in the hundredths place.   67.03

10. Circle the name of the shape.

    parallelogram   rhombus   trapezium   

My score:

10

My time: ....
                       minutes   seconds

Minute 17

Name: .... **Date:** ....

1. Write the number in standard form:

   twelve thousand, eight hundred and eleven. ....

2. Write the missing family fact.

   $6 + 9 = 15$

   $9 + 6 = 15$

   $15 - 9 = 6$

   ☐ − ☐ = ☐

3. Circle the digit in the thousandths place.   9.463

4. Double 90. ....

5. $11 \times 9 =$ ....

6. $20 \div 8 =$ .... r ....

7. Write the value. £..............

8. Write a fraction for the shaded area. ....

9. 2 litres = ... millilitres

10. Write the measurement as shown by the arrow. ....centimetres.

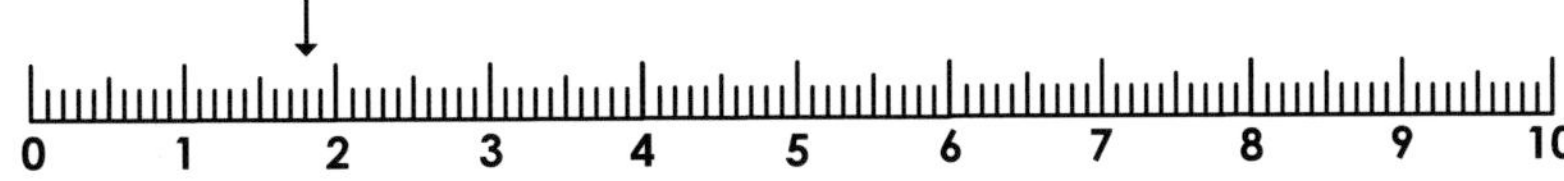

My score: ______

10

My time: ....
minutes   seconds

Minute 18

Name: .... **Date:** ....

1. 600 000 + 30 000 + 7000 + 100 + 50 + 1 = ...

2.   94
   −   48
      ....

      ....

3. Circle the digit in the tenths place.   420.177

4. Double 600. ....

5. 24 ÷ 8 = ...

6. 1 tablespoon = 20 mL   4 tablespoons = ... mL

7. How many 50-pence pieces are in 5 pounds? .... 50-pence pieces

8. The lines are perpendicular.   Circle: True   or   False

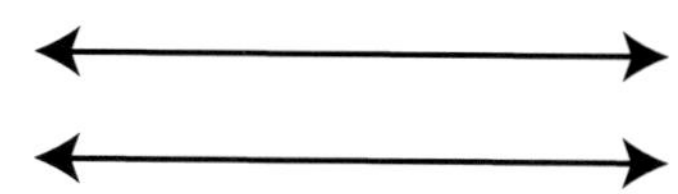

Use the pie chart to complete Questions 9 and 10.

9. Which is the most popular fruit? ....

10. Which fruit is less popular than

    apples? ....

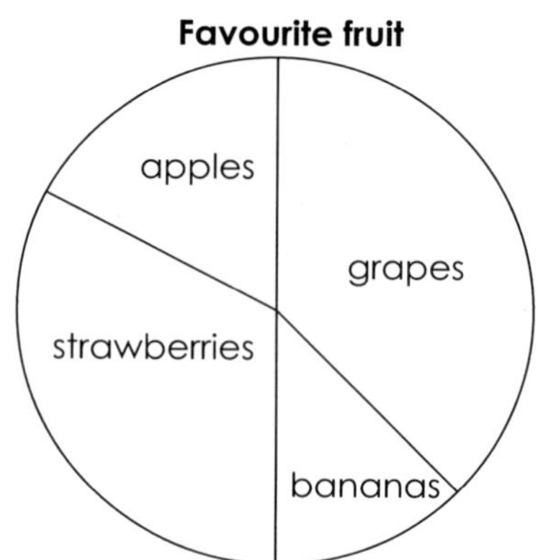

My score: ______
10

My time: ....
minutes   seconds

Minute 19

Name: .... **Date:** ....

1. Circle the digit in the millions place.   8 179 265

2.   46
   − 17
   ....

   ....

3.   9
       4
       1
   + 6
   ....

   ....

4. 6 x 7 = ...

5. Share £10.00 among 4 people. £ .... each

6. 4)‾12‾

7. Double 450. ....

8. Circle the digit in the hundredths place.   14.208

9. Write the measurement as shown by the arrow. .... centimetres

10. Circle the name of the shape.

    parallelogram   rhombus   trapezium

My score: ____ / **10**

My time: ....
               minutes   seconds

Minute 20

Name: .... **Date:** ....

1. Use <, > or =.   547 134 ⬚ 54 713

2.   93
    + 87
    ....

    ....

3. Circle the digit in the thousandths place. 13.426

4. Continue the pattern.   72, 64, 56, ..., ..., ...

5. Write the number in standard form:

   three hundred and seventy-two thousand, five hundred and twelve.

   ....

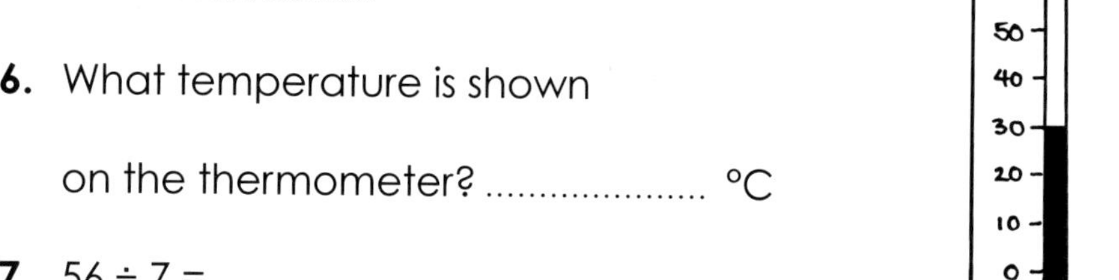

6. What temperature is shown

   on the thermometer? .... °C

7. 56 ÷ 7 = ...

8. Double 90. ....

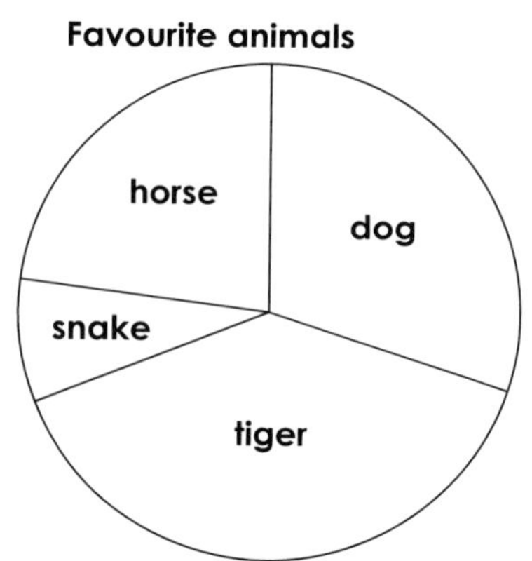

Use the pie chart to complete Questions 9 and 10.

9. Thirty per cent of the pupils said their

   favourite animal was a ....

10. What percentage of the pupils said the tiger

   was their favourite animal?

   25%   40%   70%

My score: ——— / **10**

My time: .... minutes seconds

Minute 21

Name: .... **Date:** ....

1. 5 weeks = ... days

2.
$$919 - 584$$

3. Write the number in standard form:

   one hundred and eleven thousand, six hundred and thirty-six.

   ....

4. How many legs altogether are there on 4 dogs? .... legs

5. 7 cm = ... mm

6. 48 ÷ 5 = ... r ....

7. Round 65 470 to the nearest thousand. ....

8. Continue the pattern.   200, 211, 222, ..., ...

9. Write the numbers in order from lowest to highest.

   3920   392   3092   923

   ....

10. Draw what comes next in the pattern.

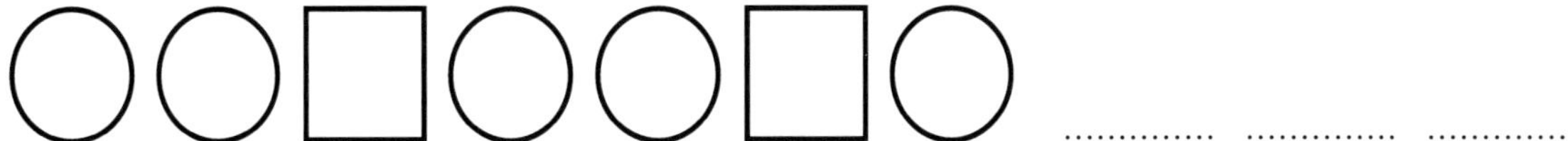

   ....

My score: $\dfrac{}{10}$

My time: ....
                 minutes   seconds

Minute 22

Name: .... **Date:** ....

1. 8 x 5 = ...

2. 73 ÷ 3 = ... r ....

3. Write an equation for 'the sum of 102 and 60'. ....

4.   30 571
   + 12 619

   ....

5. Does 37 ÷ 18 mean '18 less than 37'?   Circle: Yes   or   No

Use the line graph to complete Questions 6 and 7.

6. On which quiz did Chas do the best?

   ....

7. Did Chas' score **improve** or **decline** between quizzes 1 and 2?

   ....

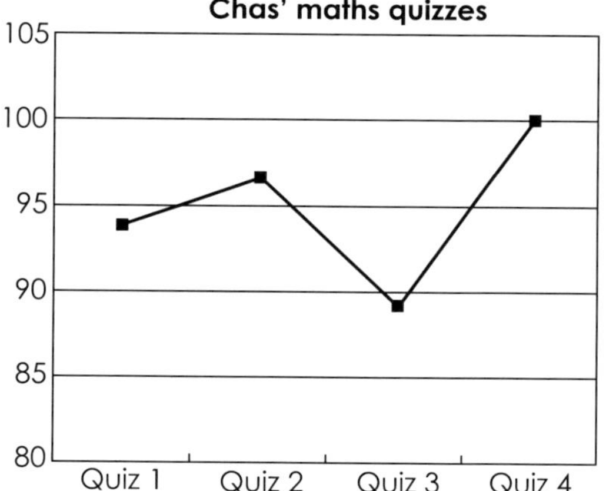

8. Use <, > or =.

   728 109 [   ] 782 109

9. 1 cup = 250 mL

   .... cups = 1 L (1000 mL)

10.   1
         4
         9
   +   6
   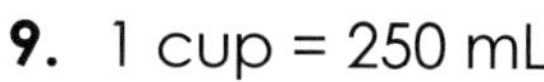

   ....

Minute 23

Name: .... **Date:** ....

1. Round 11.64 to the nearest tenth.

    Circle the answer.   11.6   11.7

2. 6 000 000 + 30 000 + 70 = ...

3. How many eyes altogether on 8 children? .... eyes

4.   200
    –   73
       ....

       ....

5. Write the missing family fact.

    2 + 3 = 5
    3 + 2 = 5
    5 – 2 = 3

    ....

6. £50.00 – £35.00 ....

7. What temperature is shown on the thermometer? .... °C

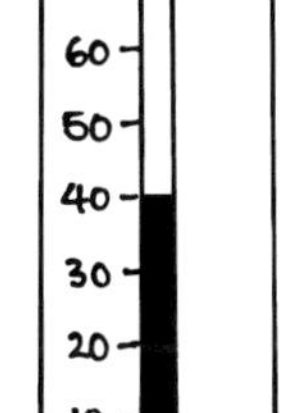

8. Round 2 540 812 to the nearest million. Circle the answer.

    2 000 000   3 000 000

9. 8 + n = 20;

    therefore, n = ...

10.   £5.24
     +   £2.72
       ....

       ....

<table>
<tr><td>My score:</td><td>10</td><td>My time:</td><td>.......................... minutes</td><td>.......................... seconds</td></tr>
</table>

Minute 24

Name: .... **Date:** ....

1. Write the numbers in order from lowest to highest.

   8.54   8.45   8.05   8.40

   ....

2.   81
     + 15
     ....

     ....

3. Round 16.1513 to the nearest thousandth. Circle the answer.

   16.151   16.152

4. 10 x 11 = ...

5.   3972
     – 1023
     ....

     ....

6. Write the measurement as shown by the arrow. .... millimetres

7. Write the value of the bold digit. 9 8**6**2 467   ....

8. Write the missing family fact.

   3 x 8 = 24
   8 x 3 = 24
   24 ÷ 8 = 3

   ....

9.   £7.45
     – £6.04
     ....

     ....

10. Draw what comes next in the pattern.   ....

My score: _______
10

My time: ....
   minutes   seconds

Maths minutes

www.prim-ed.com   Prim-Ed Publishing®

Minute 25

Name: .... **Date:** ....

1. Circle the lowest number.   39 725   94 387   49 747   39 279

2.   1116
    +   407
    ....

    ....

3. 10 x 12 = ...

4. Round 70 954 to the nearest hundred. Circle the answer.

   70 900   71 000

5. How many points did Team 5 score? .... points

Team	1	2	3	4	5	6
Points	3	9	27	81		729

6. 121 ÷ 11 = ...

Use the pie chart to complete Questions 7 to 9.

7. What is the most common number of

   family members? .... members

8. What percentage of people have

   3 family members? ....

9. Just 6% of families have how many

   family members? .... members

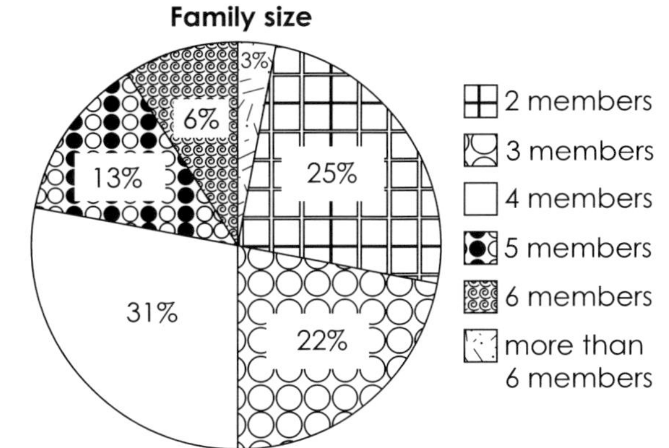

10. Write the numbers in order from highest to lowest.

    14.92   19.42   14.29   19.24

    ....

My score: ______   10

My time: ....
         minutes   seconds

Minute 26

Name: .... **Date:** ....

1.   857
      − 432
    ....

    ....

2. Circle the digit in the hundredths place. 0.54

3. Write the missing family fact.

    $5 + 6 = 11$
    $11 − 5 = 6$
    $11 − 6 = 5$

    ....

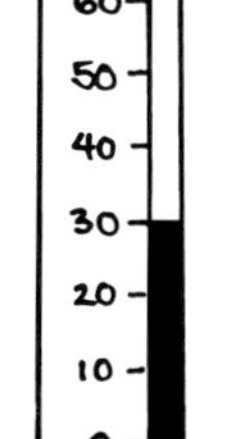

4. 90 x 5 = ...

5. What temperature is shown

    on the thermometer? ....°C

6. When you multiply any number by 0, the product is 0.

    Circle: True   or   False

7. Use <, >, or =. 8 015 943 .... 8 019 435

8. 26 ÷ 4 = ... r ....

9. 10 + a = 25;

    therefore, a = ...

10. Is the dashed line a line of symmetry? Circle: Yes or No

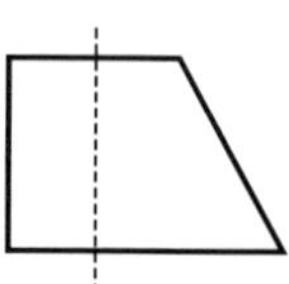

My score: ______ / **10**

My time: ....
minutes   seconds

Minute 27

Name: .... **Date:** ....

1.   620
   + 921
   ....

2. Round 0.**3**58 to the **bold** place.

   Circle the answer.   0.3   0.4

3. 10 x 14 = ...

4. £50.00 – £32.00 = ...

5.   8653
   – 6228
   ....

6. Write the missing family fact.

   6 x 9 = 54
   9 x 6 = 54
   54 ÷ 9 = 6

   ....

7. 19 L = ... mL

8. Is 37 a prime number or a composite number? ....

9. 39 ÷ 3 = ...

10. Circle the name of the triangle.

   isosceles   equilateral   scalene   right-angle

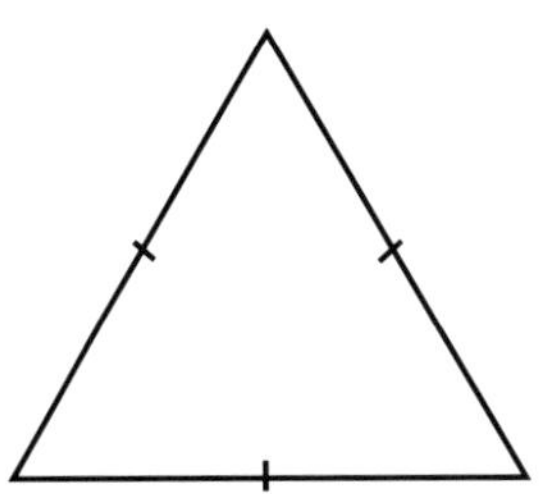

My score: $\dfrac{\quad}{10}$ **My time:** ....
                                          minutes   seconds

Minute 28

Name: .... **Date:** ....

1. Circle the digit in the tenths place.   4.032

2. 10 x 9 = ...

3.   £2.04
    − £1.53
    ....

    ....

4. $x - 25 = 10$;

    therefore, x = ...

5.   8
          5
          3
    +   2
    ....

    ....

6. 28 ÷ 2 = ...

7. All sides are congruent in a scalene triangle.   Circle: True   or   False

8.   127
    −   96
    ....

    ....

9. Write the numbers in order from highest to lowest.

    0.013   0.13   1.30   0.31

    ....

10. Write a fraction for the number of shaded figures. ....

Minute 29

Name: .... **Date:** ....

1. Write the missing family fact.

    $7 + 5 = 12$
    $12 - 7 = 5$
    $12 - 5 = 7$

    ....

2.   2197
    +   1557
    ....

    ....

3. Can 226 be divided evenly by 9?   Circle: Yes   or   No

4. What temperature is shown

    on the thermometer? ....°C

5.   40.42
    –   17.19
    ....

    ....

6. Circle the digit in the thousandths place.   4.580

7. £50.00 – £20.50 = ...

8.   £3.70
    –   £2.18
    ....

    ....

9. Circle the name of the triangle.

    isosceles   equilateral   scalene   right-angle

10. $n + 10 = 25$;

    therefore, $n =$ ....

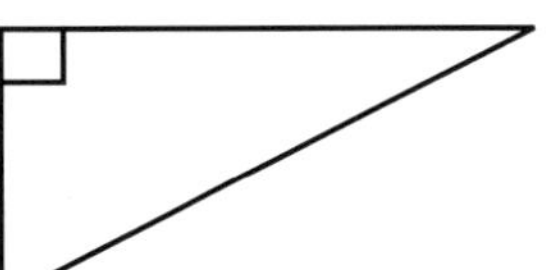

My score: $\dfrac{\quad\quad}{10}$ **My time:** ....

                                                         minutes   seconds

Minute 30

Name: .... **Date:** ....

1. $10 \times 10 =$ ....

2. $8\overline{)144} =$ ....

3. $37 + y = 87$;

   therefore, $y =$ ....

4. Round 3.1**0**1 to the bold place. Circle the answer.   3.1   3.11

5.   £13.07
   + £ 0.51
   ....

   ....

6. Write the digit in the ten thousands place.   76 543 ....

7. 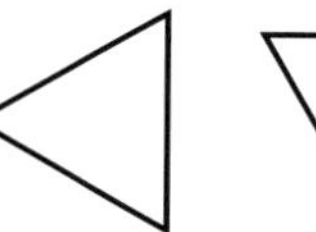 = 1000 kilograms

   4 tonnes = ... kilograms

8. Write the missing family fact.

   $8 + 5 = 13$
   $5 + 8 = 13$
   $13 - 5 = 8$

   ....

9. Are the triangles congruent? ....

10. Write the numbers in order from lowest to highest.

    16.15   15.16   16.51   16.01

    ....

My score: $\dfrac{}{10}$ **My time:** .... minutes .... seconds

Minute 31

Name: .... **Date:** ....

1. 525
    + 326
    ....

    ....

2. Circle the digit in the hundredths place.   73.15

3. 1 000 000 + 70 000 + 400 + 9 = ...

4. 50 x 7 = ...

5. Write the name of the angle. ....

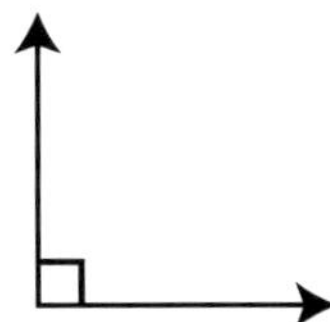

6. How much money is (1 x £1) + (3 x 50p) + (1 x 20p) + (3 x 10p)? ....

7. Write the missing family fact.

    4 x 8 = 32
    8 x 4 = 32
    32 ÷ 8 = 4

    ....

8. 4076
    − 2633
    ....

    ....

9. 8 metres – 5 metres = ... metres

10. $8 \times n = 56$;

    therefore, n = ...

My score: $\dfrac{}{10}$ **My time:** ....
                                            minutes   seconds

Minute 32

Name: .... **Date:** ....

1. 5 20-pence pieces = ... 10-pence pieces

2. 20 x 9 = ...

3. Can a line of symmetry be drawn on the shape?
   Circle: Yes   or   No

4. $1\frac{1}{2}$ cm = ... mm

5. 16 litres – 7 litres = ... litres

6.   751
   –   39
   ....

   ....

7. $x \div 8 = 3$;

   therefore, x = ...

8.   1
      9
      2
   + 8
   ....

   ....

9. Use <, > or =.

   3 052 112 .... 3 052 115

10. Draw what comes next in the pattern.

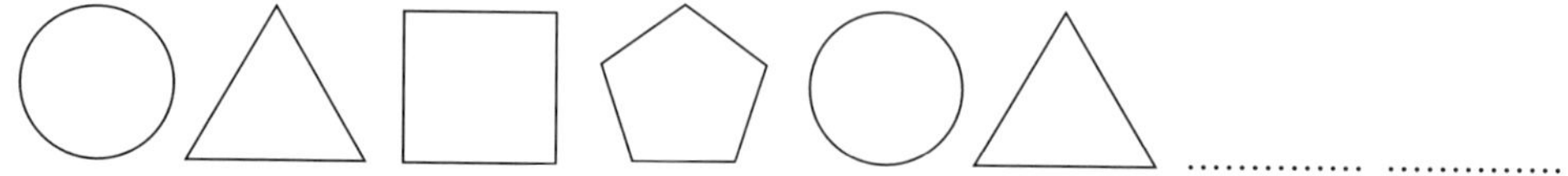

My score: $\frac{}{10}$ **My time:** ....
                                     minutes   seconds

Maths minutes

Minute 33

Name: .... **Date:** ....

1. 11 700
    + 92 798

    ....

2. Circle the digit in the tenths place.   35.418

Use the pie chart to complete Questions 3 to 5.

3. Which season is the least favourite? ....

4. What is the title of the chart? ....

   ....

5. Which two seasons are equally favoured?

   .... and ....

6. Write the missing family fact.

   4 x 8 = 32   8 x 4 = 32

   32 ÷ 8 = 4   ....

7. 6)‾96‾

8. 100 x 30 = ...

9. Write the numbers in order from highest to lowest.

   10.30   10.03   1.03   10.33

   ....

10. Circle coins that equal £0.65.

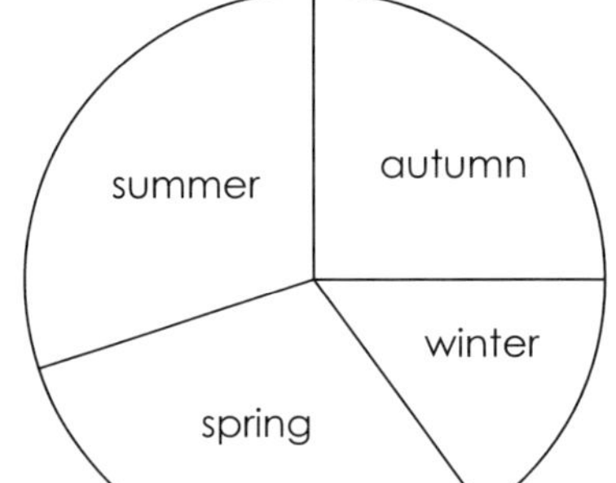

Favourite seasons

My score: ____
          10

My time: ....
                  minutes   seconds

Minute 34

Name: .... **Date:** ....

1. $6\frac{1}{4}$ km = ... m

2. $14 + a = 18$;
   therefore, $a =$ ....

3. $3\overline{)216}$

4. Circle the digit in the thousandths place.   1.23046

5.   16.02
   $-$ 3.40
   ....

   ....

6. $60 \times 80 =$ ....

7. If you buy 30 items, how many will you get for free? .... free items

Bought items	5	10	15	20		
Free items	1	3	5	7		

8.   £7.97
   $+$ £1.36
   ....

   ....

9. Use <, > or =.   308 912 .... 380 911

10. What is the perimeter of the square? .... units

4

Minute 35

Name: .... **Date:** ....

1. 2050 g = ... kg

2. $\begin{array}{r} 531 \\ -\ \ 89 \\ \hline \end{array}$

   ....

3. 1 cup = 250 mL

   8 cups = ... L

4. 84 ÷ 7 = ...

5. Draw what comes next in the pattern.

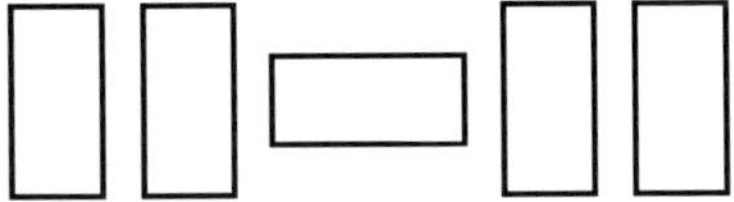

   ....

6. 56 ÷ n = 7;

   therefore, n = ...

7. 70 x 60 = ...

8. £100 – £47 = £ ....

9. 4.14 + 5.12 = ...

10. Placed on the number line, is $\frac{1}{7}$ closest to 0, $\frac{1}{2}$ or 1? ....

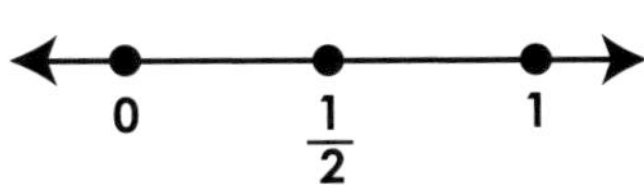

My score: $\dfrac{\quad}{10}$

My time: ....
   minutes   seconds

Minute 36

Name: .... **Date:** ....

1. Round 16.13 to the bold place. ....

2. Underline the product of 17 x 6.

   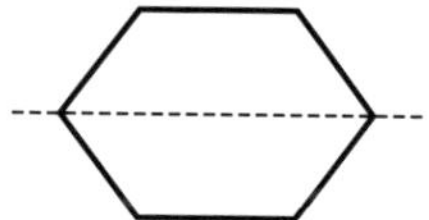
   617   102   176   201

3. Is the dashed line a line of symmetry?

   Circle: Yes   or   No

4. 7.5 cm = ... mm

5.   1127
    +   221
    ....

    ....

6. How many 20p coins make up £3? ....

7. $9\overline{)171}$

8.   £7.13
    +   £0.15
    ....

    ....

9. Circle the name of the triangle.

   right-angle   isosceles   scalene

10. $46 - b = 30$;

    therefore, $b =$ ....

My score: ____ / **10**   My time: ....
                                         minutes   seconds

Minute 37

Name: ....   **Date:** ....

1. Write the missing family fact.

   $3 \times 6 = 18$ $18 \div 6 = 3$

   $18 \div 3 = 6$ ....

2.   £10.91
    − £ 9.25
    ....

    ....

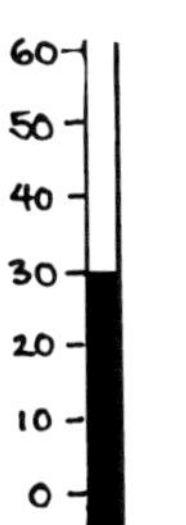

3. What would the temperature be if it fell 15 degrees? ....°C

4. $1\ t = 1000\ kg$ $6\frac{1}{2}\ t =$ .... kg

5. $900 \div 90 =$ ....

6. If placed on the number line, is $\frac{11}{12}$ closer to 0, $\frac{1}{2}$ or 1? ....

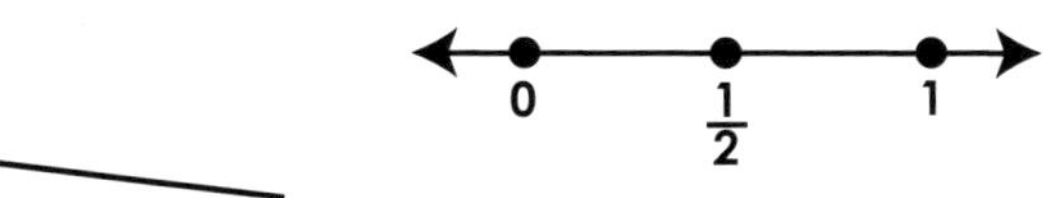

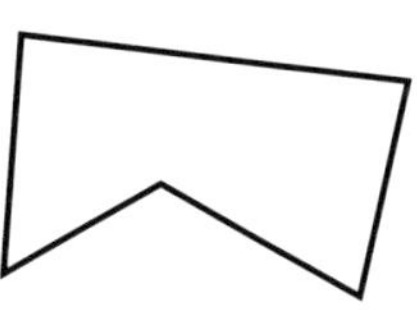

7. Is the shape symmetrical?

   Circle: Yes or No

8.   £6.85
    + £2.03
    ....

    ....

9. Circle the digit in the hundredths place.   16.39

10.   90 776
    − 87 644
    ....

    ....

My score: ______
            10

My time: ....
                minutes   seconds

Minute 38

Name: .... **Date:** ....

1. What is the perimeter of the rectangle? .... units   **2** [**5**]

2. Write the numbers in order from highest to lowest.

    0.18   0.81   0.01   0.08

    ....

3.   85
   x   4
   ....

   ....

4.   6
    7
    3
 + 4
   ....

   ....

5. $60 \div 4 =$ ....

6. 13 km = ... m

7. How much time is it from 8.00 am to 11.30 am? .... hours .... minutes

8. $19 + n = 37$;

   therefore, $n =$ ....

9. Circle the name of the triangle.

   equilateral   isosceles   scalene

10. Draw what comes next in the pattern.

   ....

My score: $\dfrac{}{10}$ **My time:** .... minutes .... seconds

Minute 39

Name: .... **Date:** ....

1. How many 20p coins make up £2.40? ....

2. 186
   x   3
   ....

   ....

3. 211.60
   −   16.12
   ....

   ....

4. 45 g = ... kg   (1000 g = 1 kg)

5. Circle the digit in the tenths place.   25.16

6. 813
   + 529
   ....

   ....

7. Circle the name of the angle.

   acute   right   obtuse

Use the bar graph to complete Questions 8 to 10.

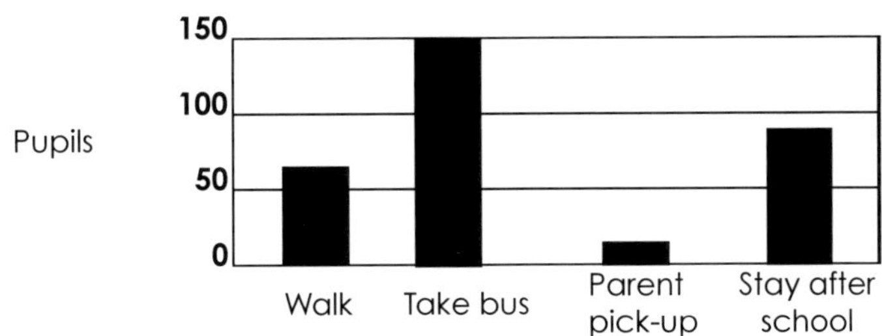

8. Do more pupils walk home or stay after school? ....

9. How many pupils take the bus? .... pupils

10. What is the least common after-school transportation? ....

My score: ______
10

My time: ....
                        minutes   seconds

Minute 40

Name: .... **Date:** ....

1. $\begin{aligned} 9753 \\ -\ 8108 \end{aligned}$

2. Circle the digit in the thousandths place.   7.6314

3. $\begin{aligned} 190 \\ \times\ \ 7 \end{aligned}$

4. If placed on a number line, is $\frac{19}{20}$ closer to 0, $\frac{1}{2}$, or 1? ....

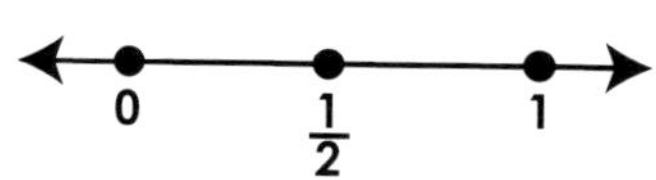

5. How many pupils could ride on 4 buses? .... pupils

Pupils	48	96	144	
Buses	1	2	3	4

6. $\begin{aligned} 20.16 \\ +\ 15.10 \end{aligned}$

7. $240 \div 60 =$ ....

8. What is the perimeter of the square? .... units

9. 4 hours and 15 minutes – 1 hour and 5 minutes =

     .... hour(s) and .... minute(s)

10. $70 - n = 38$;

     therefore, $n =$ ....

My score: $\frac{\quad}{10}$ **My time:** .... minutes   .... seconds

Minute 41

Name: .... **Date:** ....

1. £22.09
    + £ 7.35
    ....

    ....

2. Round 0.2**0**9 to the bold place. ....

3. 90 ÷ 6 = ...

4. 31 m and 80 cm – 3 m and 60 cm = ... m .... cm.

5. A scalene triangle has no congruent sides.   Circle: True   or   False

6. £10.09
    – £ 7.13
    ....

    ....

7. $7 \times n = 84$;

    therefore, n = ...

8. 2.7 m = ... cm   (1 m = 100 cm)

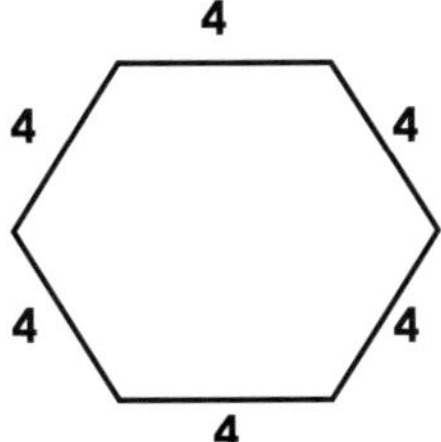

9. What is the perimeter of the shape? .... units

10. Circle how many lines of symmetry the shape has.   1   2   3   4

My score: ______ / **10**   **My time:** ....
minutes   seconds

Minute 42

Name: .... **Date:** ....

1. $540 \div 6 =$ ....

2. A number is divisible by 3 if the sum of its digits is divisible by 3.

   Circle: True or False

3. How many apples are in 1 dozen? .... apples

4. £4.73
   x   8
   ....

   ....

5. $15 \times n = 45$;

   therefore, $n =$ ....

6. $0.14 + 16.15 =$ ....

Use the table to complete Questions 7 to 8.

Roosters	1	2	3	4	5	6	7	8
Chickens	25	50	75					

7. If there are 5 roosters, how many chickens are there? .... chickens

8. If there are 200 chickens, how many roosters are there? .... roosters

9. What would the temperature be

   if it decreased by 8 degrees? ....°C

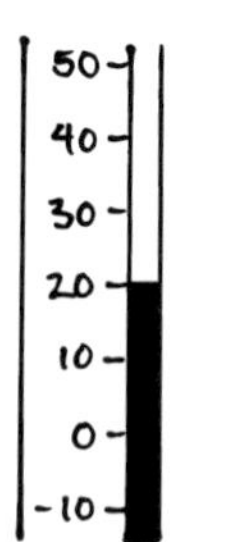

10. rate = 60 kilometres/hour

    If a car travels for 2 hours, how many kilometres will it travel? .... kilometres

---

My score: $\dfrac{\quad}{10}$ **My time:** ....

                                                          minutes   seconds

Minute 43

Name: .... **Date:** ....

1. $7\overline{)1750}$

2.   £9.83
   − £8.92
   ....

   ....

3. A number is divisible by 4 if the last two digits are divisible by 4.

   Circle: True or False

4. Circle how many lines of symmetry the shape has.

   1   2   3   4

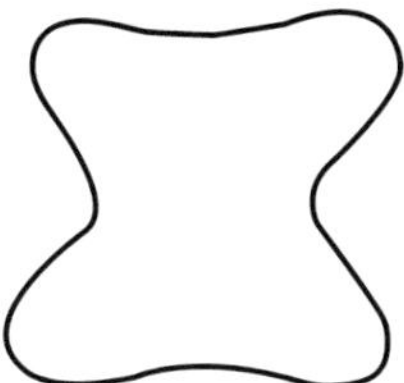

5. Use <, > or =.

   14 760 [____] 14 706

6. £100 − £39.75 = ...

7. Round 12 892 to the nearest hundred. ....

8. Circle the name of the angle.   acute   right   obtuse

9. 60 ÷ 3 = ...

10. 23 x b = 92;
    therefore, b = ...

Minute 44

Name: .... **Date:** ....

1. £100 – £44.50 = ...

2. £3.50
    x 6

    ....

3. Double 160. ....

Use the table to complete Questions 4 and 5.

Red ribbons	4	6	8	10	12	14	16	18
Blue ribbons	7	14	21					

4. If there are 18 red ribbons, how many blue ribbons are there? .... blue ribbons

5. If there are 42 blue ribbons, how many red ribbons are there? .... red ribbons

6. If placed on a number line, is $\frac{9}{15}$ closer to 0, $\frac{1}{2}$ or 1? ....

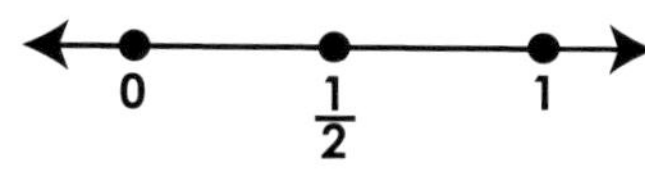

7. rate = 80 kilometres/hour

   If a bus travels for 3 hours, how many kilometres will it travel? .... kilometres

8. Write the name of the angle. ....

9. A protractor is used to measure angles. Circle: True or False

10. $4\overline{)68}$

My score: _______

10

My time: ....
minutes   seconds

Minute 45

Name: .... **Date:** ....

1. Can 1025 be evenly divided by 5?   Circle: Yes   or   No

2. 21 days = ... weeks

3. There are 42 weeks in one year.   Circle: True or False

4. Circle the shape that does not belong.

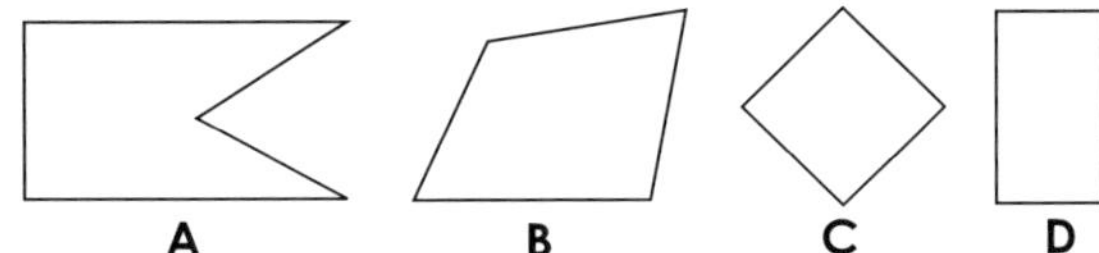

5. $6 \times n = 72$;

   therefore, n = ...

6. 125 minutes = ... hour(s) .... minute(s)

7. 0.25×10 = ...

8. Write the measurement as shown by the arrow. .... millimetres

9.   1803
    x   2
    ....

    ....

10. $9\overline{)3060}$

<table>
<tr><td>My score:</td><td>10</td><td>My time:</td><td>minutes</td><td>seconds</td></tr>
</table>

Minute 46

Name: .... **Date:** ....

1. $(1 \times 50p) + (6 \times 20p) + (3 \times 10p) =$ ....

2. £1.42
   x   4
   ....

   ....

3. $7\overline{)44.45}$

4. £50.00 – £21.90 = ...

5. $5\overline{)21}$ r.............

6. Are the two shapes congruent? 

   Circle: Yes or No

7. Circle the name of the angle.   acute   right   obtuse

   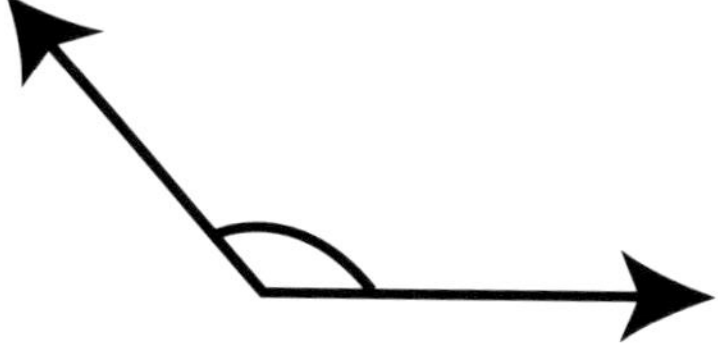

9. 6127
   x   5
   ....

   ....

9. A number is divisible by 4 if the last two digits are divisible by 4.

   Circle: True or False

10. rate = 45 kilometres/hour

    If a bus travels for 4 hours, how many kilometres will it travel? ....kilometres

---

My score: ______ / **10**

My time: ....
                    minutes   seconds

Minute 47

Name: .... **Date:** ....

1. 1000 mL = 1 L

   600 mL = ... L

2. 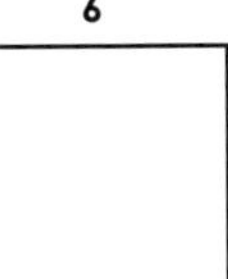 $\frac{1}{2} = \frac{}{6}$

3. £9.80
   x   5
   ....

   ....

4. The perimeter of the square is ....units.

5. 51 minutes x 3 = ... hour(s) .... minute(s)

6. Name this shape. ....

7. Circle the best estimate for the measurement of the angle. 40° 90° 170°

   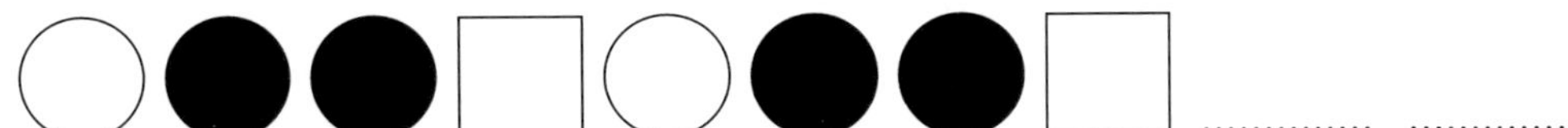

8. 17.19 – 0.20 = ...

9. 832 ÷ 4 = ...

10. Draw what comes next in the pattern.

    ....

My score: $\frac{}{10}$

My time: ....
    minutes   seconds

Minute 48

Name: .... **Date:** ....

1. $121 \div a = 11$;

   therefore, $a =$ ....

2. $\dfrac{2}{5} = \dfrac{}{15}$

3.   £1.39
   − £0.87
   ....

   ....

4. A number that is multiplied is called the factor.   Circle: True   or   False

5.   £8.18
   x   9
   ....

   ....

6. 5 hours, 10 minutes + 2 hours, 40 minutes = ... hour(s) .... minute(s)

7. What would the temperature

   be if it fell by 11 degrees? .... °C

8. When you multiply any number by 0, the product is ....

9.   £8.42
   + £3.88
   ....

   ....

10. $4\overline{)412}$

My score: $\dfrac{}{10}$ **My time:** ....

  minutes   seconds

Minute 49

Name: .... Date: ....

1. Write $\frac{12}{100}$ as a percentage. .... %

2. $4 \overline{)28.8}$

3. 1L = 1000 mL

   7.2L = ... mL

4. $Perimeter = l + w + l$ Circle: True   or   False

5. 4.04 L = ... mL

6.   407
   x   6

   ....

7. Circle how many lines of symmetry the figure has.   1   2   3   4

8. Circle the best estimate for the measurement of the angle.

   25°   90°   110°

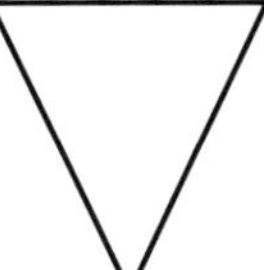

9. The names of the line segment are .... and $\overline{HG}$.

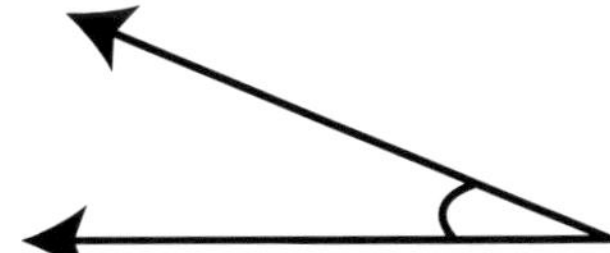

10.   616
    x   3

    ....

My score: ____ / 10   My time: ....
                                      minutes   seconds

Minute 50

Name: .... **Date:** ....

1. £30.14
    + £ 6.27
    ....

    ....

2. $\dfrac{6}{9} = \dfrac{}{27}$

3. Circle the name of the shape.   rectangle   trapezium   rhombus

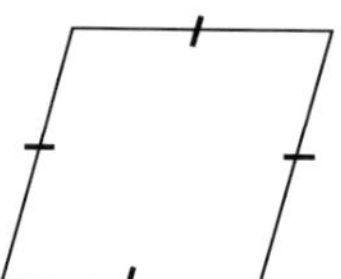

4. £2.54
    x   5
    ....

    ....

5. If the radius of a circle is 20 cm, the diameter is ....

6. 6 hours 13 minutes – 4 hours 7 minutes = ...hour(s) ....minute(s)

7. 2013
    x   9
    ....

    ....

8. . Circle the name of the angle.   acute   right   obtuse

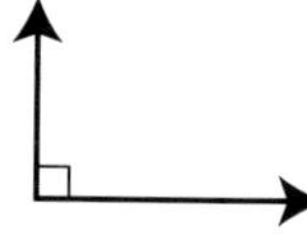

9. 8)22   r ....

10. Draw what comes next in the pattern.

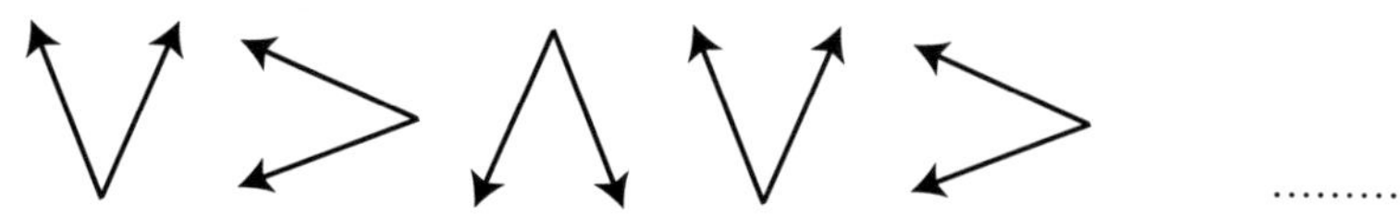

....

My score: $\dfrac{}{10}$ **My time:** ....
                                              minutes   seconds

Minute 51

Name: .... **Date:** ....

1. £4.06
   x   4
   ....

   ....

2. Round 0.**18** to the bold place. ....

3. 500 x 8 = ...

4. Write the missing family fact.

   2 x 8 = 16   8 x 2 = 16

   16 ÷ 2 = 8   ....

5. 203
   x   8
   ....

   ....

6. 1 hour 12 minutes x 3 = ...hour(s) ....minute(s)

7. This shape is an ....

8. Circle the best estimate for the measurement of the angle.   50°   90°   145°

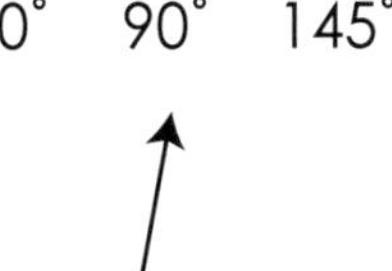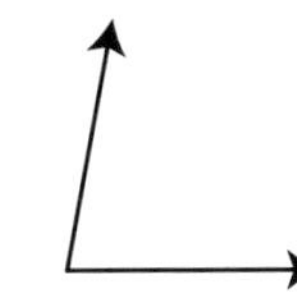

9. What is the perimeter of the shape? .... units

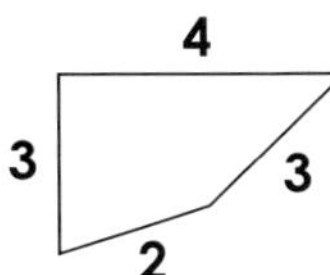

10. A shape is symmetrical if it can be divided so that both sides match.

    Circle: True or False

My score: $\dfrac{\quad\quad}{10}$ **My time:** .... minutes .... seconds

Minute 52

Name: .... **Date:** ....

1. £0.95
   x   9
   ....

2. Is the shape symmetrical? Circle: Yes or No

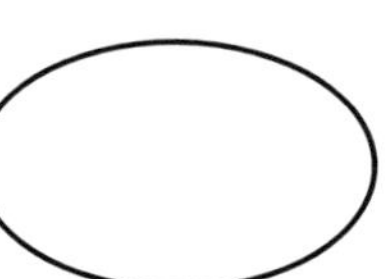

3. 0.008 x 9 = ...

4. 60 x 70 = ...

5. $7\overline{)434}$

6.   20.11
   +   6.12
   ....

7. rate = 40 kilometres/hour

   If a train travels for 6 hours, how many kilometres will it travel? .... kilometres

8.   9341
   x   2
   ....

9. Does the letter **X** have a line of symmetry? Circle: Yes or No

10. Circle the name of the triangle.

    equilateral   right-angle   isosceles

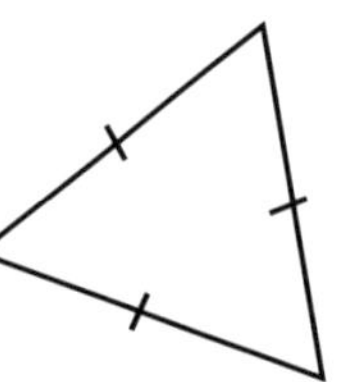

My score: _______
10

My time: ....
minutes   seconds

www.prim-ed.com   Prim-Ed Publishing®

Minute 53

Name: .... **Date:** ....

1. $\dfrac{1}{4} = \dfrac{}{28}$

2. Circle the name of the figure. 

   rhombus   parallelogram   trapezium

3. $(3 \times 10p) + (1 \times 20p) + (4 \times 5p) = £$.............

4. Does the letter **D** have a line of symmetry? ....

5. rate = 10 kilometres/hour

   If Jake rode his bike for $1\frac{1}{2}$ hours, how many kilometres did he travel?

   .... kilometres

6. $\begin{array}{r} 56 \\ \times\ \ 3 \\ \hline \\ \hline \end{array}$

7. What would the temperature be if it

   increased by 7 degrees? ....°C

8. $2\overline{)0.036}$

Write the word that completes each sentence.

9. The answer in a subtraction problem is called the ....

   difference   quotient   dividend

10. The answer in a division problem is called the ....

    difference   quotient   dividend

My score: $\dfrac{\quad\quad}{10}$ **My time:** .... minutes   .... seconds

Minute 54

Name: .... **Date:** ....

1. $\dfrac{2}{3} = \dfrac{}{15}$

2. £8.21
   x   4
   ....

   ....

3.   10.12
   +   0.03
   ....

   ....

4. What is the perimeter of the square? ....units

   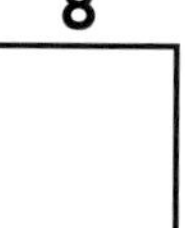

5. 1520 ÷ 5 = ...

6. 7 minutes x 9 = ...hour(s) ....minute(s)

7.   8.1
   x 0.2
   ....

   ....

8. Circle the name of the angle.   acute   right   obtuse

   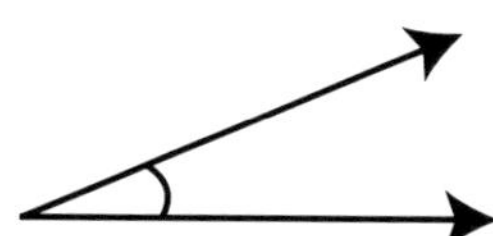

9. A cube has ....faces.

10. The point where three or more edges meet on a solid figure is called a vertex.

    Circle: True or False

    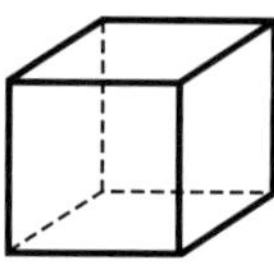

<table>
<tr><td>My score:</td><td>10</td><td>My time:</td><td>.................... minutes</td><td>.................... seconds</td></tr>
</table>

Minute 55

Name: .... **Date:** ....

1. Round 17.12 to the bold place. ....

2. 20.09 x 10 = ...

3. Write $\frac{14}{100}$ as a percentage. ....%

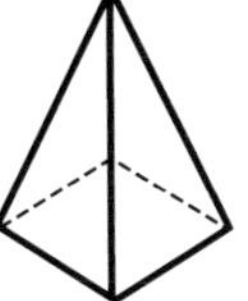

4. A square pyramid has .... vertices.

5. $8\overline{)872}$

6. Is the shape symmetrical? ....

7. $\begin{array}{r} 4110 \\ \times \quad 8 \\ \hline \end{array}$

   ....

8. Name this solid shape. ....

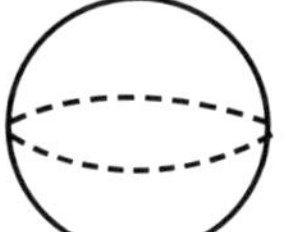

9. Circle the name of the triangle.

   equilateral   isosceles   scalene

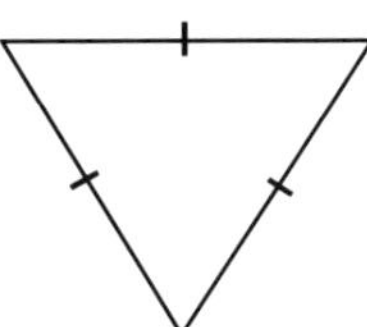

10. Circle the name of an endless flat surface.

    ray   plane   line   point

My score: $\frac{\quad}{10}$

My time: ....
minutes   seconds

Minute 56

Name: .... **Date:** ....

1. Write $\frac{46}{100}$ as a percentage. .... %

2. 80 cm = 0. .... m

3. 2.1 x 10 = ...

4. The two names of the line segment are $\overline{CD}$ and ....

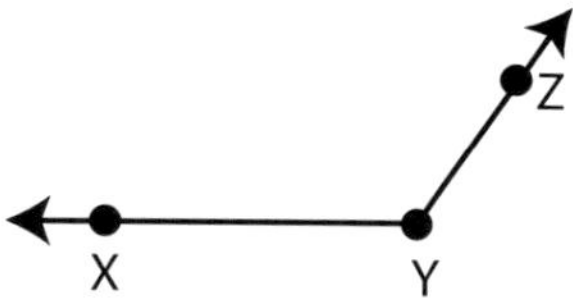

For Questions 5 to 7, write the correct word to complete each sentence.

> point   line   ray   plane   line segment

5. A .... is an endless flat surface.

6. A .... is part of a line with one endpoint.

7. An exact location is called a ....

8. 45 minutes x 2 = ... hour(s) .... minutes

9. Two names of the angle are $\angle XYZ$ and $\angle$.............

10.   204
    x   5
    ....

    ....

My score: $\frac{}{10}$

My time: ....
             minutes   seconds

Minute 57

Name: .... **Date:** ....

1. You measure temperature with a thermometer.   Circle: True   or   False

2. A right angle measures ....°.

3.   0.713
    −   0.008

    ....

4. rate = 80 kilometres/hour

   If a truck travels for $3\frac{1}{2}$ hours, how many kilometres will it travel?

   .... kilometres

5. Write the perimeter of the triangle. .... units 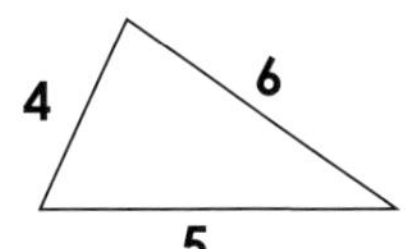

6. $9\overline{)10.08}$

7.   6018
    x   6

    ....

8. Circle the best estimate for the measurement of the angle.   19°   90°   125°

9. Factors are numbers that are multiplied to get a product.

   Circle: True   or   False

10. The distance around a polygon is called the ....

My score: _____
10

My time: ....
                    minutes   seconds

Minute 58

Name: .... **Date:** ....

1. $9\overline{)45.72}$

2. $(2 \times 50p) + (4 \times 20p) + (5 \times 5p) = £$............

3. $6\overline{)1602}$

4. Is the shape symmetrical?   Circle: Yes or No

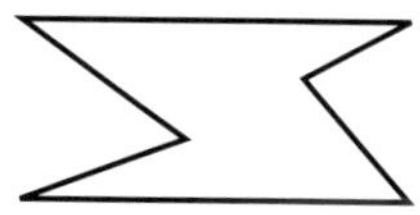

5.   17.11
   x   2
   ....

6. 20 minutes x 5 = ... hour(s) .... minute(s)

7. The two names of the angle are ∠LMN and ∠..............

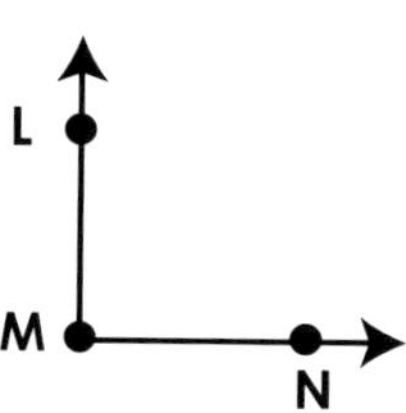

8. The number of square units needed to cover a region is called its area.

    Circle: True or False

9.   39
   x 4
   ....

10.   £8.26
   − £7.31
   ....

My score: $\dfrac{}{10}$

My time: .... minutes .... seconds

Minute 59

Name: .... **Date:** ....

1. £9.20
   x   6

   ....

2. 15.13 – 11.11 = ...

3. $\dfrac{3}{7} = \dfrac{9}{\boxed{}}$

4. $5\overline{)700}$

5. 27
   x 3

   ....

6. Circle the correct answer. The lines are: parallel   perpendicular.

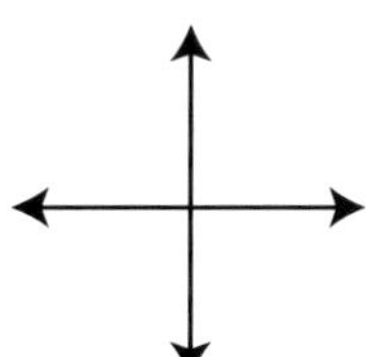

Use <, > or = to complete Questions 7 to 8.

7. $\dfrac{1}{2} \boxed{} \dfrac{1}{5}$

8. $\dfrac{3}{4} \boxed{} \dfrac{9}{12}$

9. Write the measurement as shown by the arrow. .... cm

10. A fraction names part of a whole. Circle: True or False

My score: ____ / **10**

My time: ....
               minutes   seconds

Minute 60

Name: .... **Date:** ....

1. Write $\frac{75}{100}$ as a percentage. ....%

2. Write 0.5 as a fraction. ....

3.
$$\begin{array}{r} 937 \\ \times\ \ \ 3 \\ \hline \\ \hline \end{array}$$

4. $\frac{3}{8} = \frac{}{40}$

5. 3 hours 16 minutes + 1 hour 30 minutes = ... hour(s) .... minute(s)

6. Write three-tenths as a decimal. ....

7. Circle the name of the angle. acute right obtuse

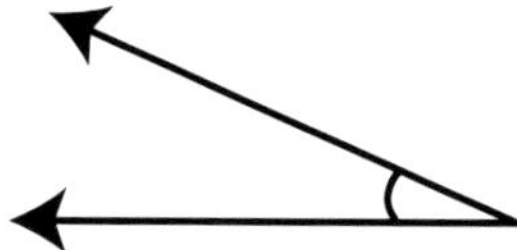

Use the bar graph to complete Questions 8 to10.

8. What is the pupils' favourite book genre? ....

9. How many pupils prefer fantasies? .... pupils

10. How many more pupils like humour than like realistic fiction? .... more pupils

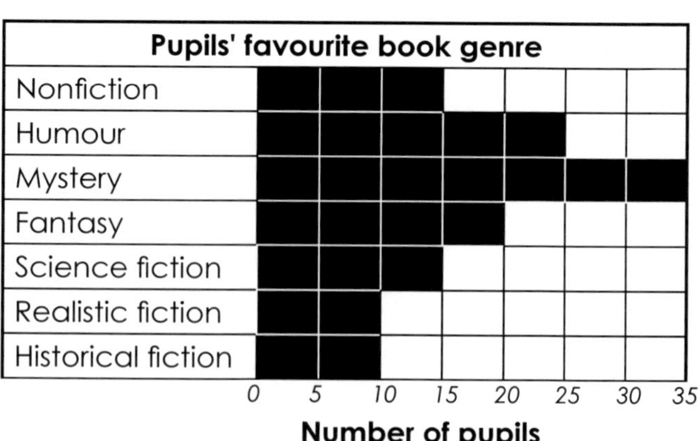

My score: $\frac{}{10}$

My time: ....
minutes   seconds

Minute 61

Name: .... **Date:** ....

1. $7\overline{)12.6}$

2. $\begin{array}{r} £5.67 \\ - \ £5.40 \\ \hline \end{array}$

   ....

3. Circle the best estimate for the measurement of the angle.

   70°   90°   150°

   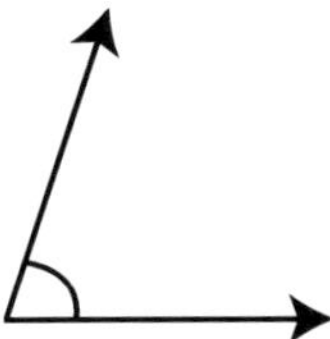

4. Write the next number in the pattern.   0.2, 0.4, 0.8, 0.16, 0.32, ...

5. $n \div 9 = 3$;

   therefore, $n =$ ....

6. 30 minutes x 6 = ... hour(s) .... minute(s)

7. $2\frac{5}{6} - 1\frac{1}{6} = 1\frac{\square}{6} = 1\frac{\square}{\square}$

8. $\begin{array}{r} 17.190 \\ + \ 3.414 \\ \hline \end{array}$

   ....

9. What is the perimeter of the shape? .... units

   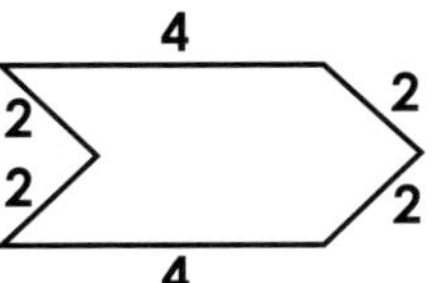

10. Is $\overline{OP}$ the radius, the centre or the diameter of the circle?

    ....

    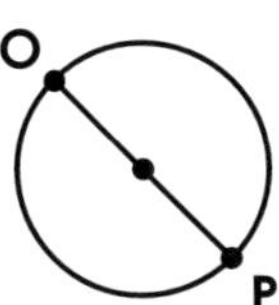

My score: $\dfrac{}{10}$ **My time:** ....

minutes   seconds

Minute 62

Name: .... **Date:** ....

1. Write what comes next in the pattern.   1.2, 2.4, 4.8 ....

2.   £1.38
     x   8
     ....

     ....

3. 7.25 L = ... mL   (1 L = 1000 mL)

4. Is the shape symmetrical? ....

5.   6.7
     x 0.3
     ....

     ....

6. 7)‾721

7. Round 3.47 to the nearest one. ....

8. $1\frac{5}{6} + 1 = \boxed{}\frac{}{6}$

9. Circle the name of the triangle.

   equilateral   isosceles   scalene   

10. rate = 60 kilometres/hour

    If a train travels for $4\frac{1}{2}$ hours, how many kilometres will it travel? .... kilometres

---

My score: ______
10

My time: ....
minutes   seconds

Minute 63

Name: .... **Date:** ....

1. £5.01
   x   7
   ....

2.   5.203
   − 4.145
   ....

3. Round 2.053 to the nearest hundredth. ....

4. 1.76 x 100 = ...

5. Circle the name of this shape.   ellipse   circle 

6. 420 ÷ 6

   Circle the answer.   50   60   70

7. Circle the best estimate for the measurement of the angle.

   45°   90°   170°

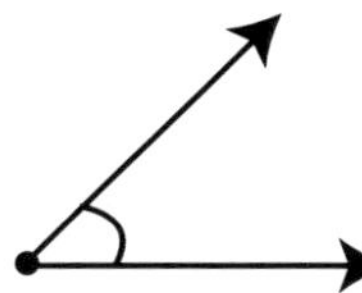

8. 2$\overline{)1496}$

9. $\frac{3}{4} - \frac{1}{4}$ = ...

10. Write $\frac{3}{100}$ as a percentage. ....%

My score: $\frac{}{10}$ **My time:** ....
                                              minutes   seconds

Minute 64

Name: .... **Date:** ....

1. $33 \div 4 =$ .... r ....

2. Use <, > or =.

   0.5 .... 0.2

3. $2.62 + 1.4 =$ ....

4. $8\overline{)2400}$

5. Circle the digit in the hundredths place. 14.027

6. Write the decimal for 2 hundredths. ....

7. Circle the name of the triangle.   equilateral   scalene   isosceles

8. $\frac{1}{7} + \frac{4}{7} =$ ....

9. $\begin{array}{r} 2.5 \\ \times\ 2 \\ \hline \end{array}$

   ....

10. What is the perimeter of the shape? .... units

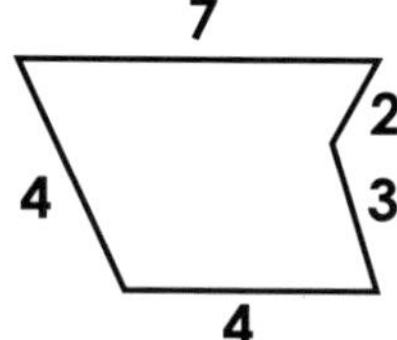

My score: $\dfrac{}{10}$ **My time:** ....

minutes   seconds

Minute 65

Name: .... **Date:** ....

1. Write $\frac{64}{100}$ as a percentage. ....%

2. 4200 ÷ 70 = ...

3.   £2.43
    x 5
    ....

    ....

4. 6.5 kg = ... g   (1 kg = 1000 g)

5. Is the shape symmetrical? ....

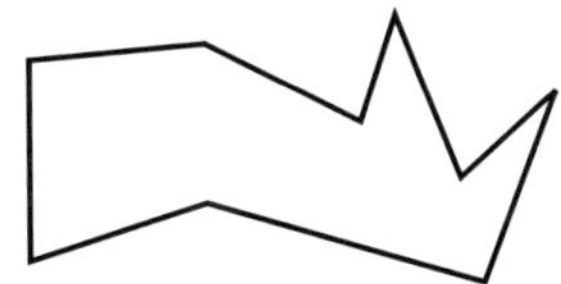

6. 8.75 x 1000 = ...

7. 3)̅1̅5̅6̅

8. Circle the name of the marked angle.

   acute   right-angle   obtuse

9. Before adding them, change the fractions so they have the same denominator.

   $\frac{1}{4} + \frac{3}{8}$ $\frac{1}{4}\left(\frac{\square}{8}\right) + \frac{3}{8} = \frac{\square}{\square}$

10. 40 minutes x 2 = ... hour(s) .... minute(s)

My score: $\frac{\qquad}{10}$ **My time:** .... minutes .... seconds

Minute 66

Name: .... **Date:** ....

1. £7.36
   x   3

   ....

2. $\frac{1}{2} = \frac{\boxed{}}{12}$

3.   0.19
   x   6

   ....

4. What is the perimeter of the shape? .... units

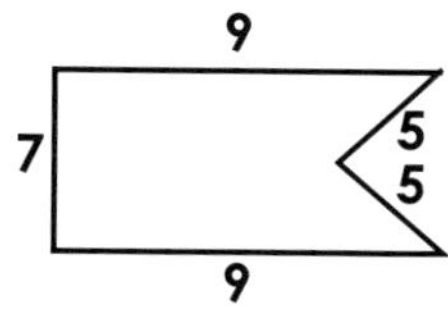

5. $\frac{5}{7} - \frac{3}{7} =$ ....

6. What is $\frac{3}{4}$ as a percentage? Circle the answer.   25%   50%   75%

7. (4 x 20p) + (7 x 50p) + (3 x 10p) = ...

8. 18 x 0 = ...

9. A right angle is .... degrees.

10. Double 99. ....

My score: $\frac{}{10}$ **My time:** ....
                                                         minutes   seconds

Minute 67

Name: .... **Date:** ....

1. £6.34
    x 3

    ....

2. 7)98

3. Write $\frac{47}{100}$ as a percentage. ....%

4. $\frac{1}{5} + \frac{2}{5}$ = ...

5. Is a diameter a line segment that passes through the centre of a circle? ....

6. A ratio is the comparison of two quantities. Circle: True or False

7. Underline the ratio of octagons to circles.   2:3   4:2   2:4

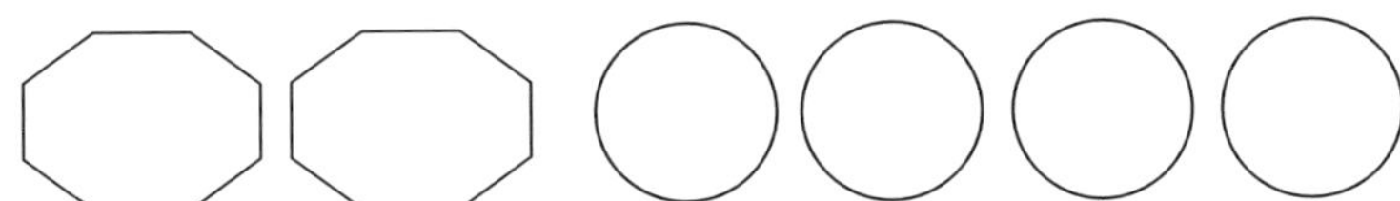

Use the line graph to complete Questions 8 to 10.

8. Did February have more sunny or rainy days? .... days

9. Which month had 20 days of rain?

    ....

10. Which months had more

    sunny days than rainy days?

    ....

    and ....

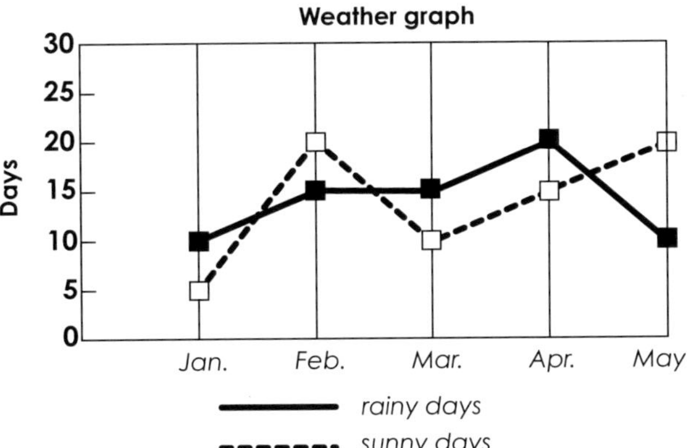

My score: $\frac{}{10}$

My time: ....
minutes   seconds

Minute 68

Name: .... Date: ....

1. What is the ratio of squares to circles? .... : ....

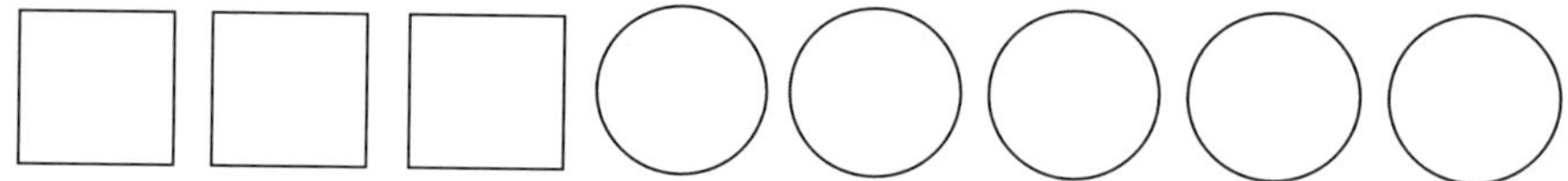

2. The two names for the line segment are $\overline{JH}$ and ....

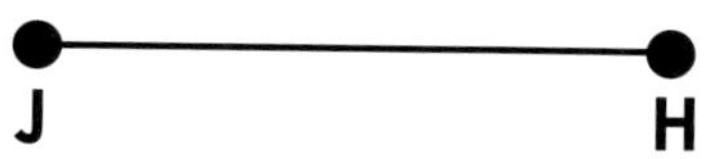

3. Volume = length x width x height ($V = l \times w \times h$)   Circle: True   or   False

4. $3\overline{)19.5}$

3. $\begin{array}{r} 1.3 \\ \times\ \ 4 \\ \hline \end{array}$

6. $3\% = \frac{3}{100} = 0.03$ Circle: True   or   False

7. $4\frac{3}{5} + 1\frac{1}{5} =$ ....

8. 5000 kg = ... t

9. Write the measurement as shown by the arrow. .... millimetres

10. $4\overline{)27.24}$

My score: $\dfrac{\quad}{10}$ My time: ....
                                        minutes   seconds

Minute 69

Name: .... **Date:** ....

1. $808 \div 8 =$ ....

2. $55\% = \frac{55}{100} = 0.55$

   Circle:　　True　　or　　False

3. Before adding them, change the fractions so they have the same denominator.

   $\frac{3}{5} + \frac{3}{10}$　　　　　$\frac{3}{5}\left(\frac{}{10}\right) + \frac{3}{10} = \frac{}{10}$

4. Circle the digit in the hundredths place.　18.07

5.　　17.190
　 $-$ 15.018
　 ....

　 ....

6. A multiple of 4 and 6 is 12.

   Circle:　　True　　or　　False

3.　　417
　 x　　5
　 ....

　 ....

8. What is the ratio of squares to triangles? .... : ....

   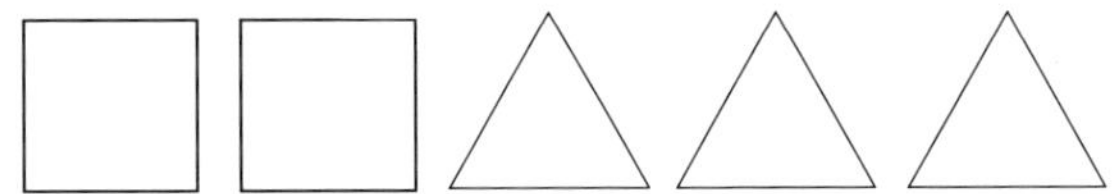

9. 0, 4, 8, 12 and 14 are all multiples of 4.　　Circle:　True　or　False

10. $\frac{2}{3}$ of 3 = ...

My score: $\frac{}{10}$　　　　**My time:** ....
　　　　　　　　　　　　　　　　　　　　　　　minutes　　　　　seconds

Minute 70

Name: .... **Date:** ....

1. Write $\frac{1}{2}$ as a percentage. ....%

2.   £6.52
    − £4.76

   ....

3. Circle the fraction equivalent to $\frac{1}{2}$. $\frac{2}{3}$ $\frac{3}{6}$ $\frac{4}{6}$

4. $\frac{1}{4}$ of 8 = ...

5. $7\frac{1}{3} - 4 =$ ....

6.   5.18
     x   7

   ....

7.   10.080
    + 0.516

   ....

8. Draw what comes next in the pattern.

....

9. 3 years = ... months

10. Circle the lowest common multiple of 3 and 6.

    6   9   2   18

My score: **10**   **My time:** ....
                                                minutes   seconds

Minute 71

Name: .... **Date:** ....

1. Circle the digit in the thousandths place.   18.6301

2. $3 + 3\frac{3}{8} =$ ....

3. Write the ratio of circles to rectangles. .... : ....

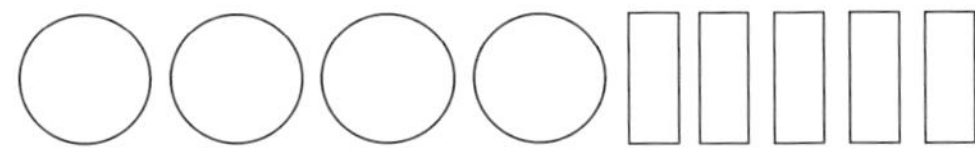

4. $\frac{1}{2}$ of 6 = ...

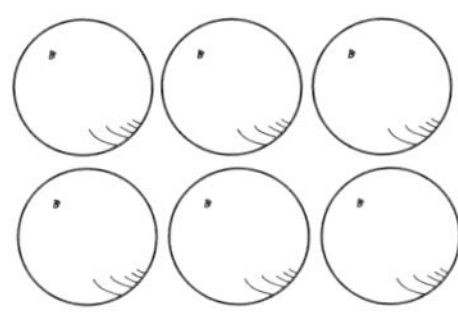

5. 15.1 x 100 = ...

6.   14.150
    − 10.018
   ....

   ....

7. Write $2\frac{3}{4}$ as an improper fraction. $\frac{\square}{4}$

8. The highest common factor of 20 and 25 is 5.   Circle: True   or   False

9. $\frac{1}{4}$ of 20 is ....

10. Write $\frac{7}{2}$ as a mixed number. $\square\frac{\square}{2}$

My score: ______ $\overline{10}$

My time: ....
minutes   seconds

Minute 72

Name: .... **Date:** ....

1. Use <, >, or =.

    0.5 .... 0.50

2. $\frac{3}{4} + \frac{2}{4}$ = ...

3.   11.60
     –   0.85
       ....

       ....

4. $\frac{1}{3}$ of 9 = ...

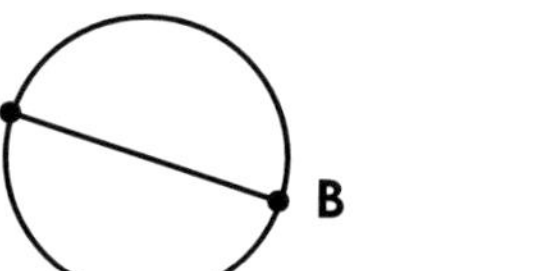

5. What is the lowest common multiple of 3 and 4? ....

6. The names of the diameter are $\overline{AB}$ and ....

multiples	
3	4
3	4
6	8
9	12
12	16
15	20

7. 20% = $\frac{}{100}$

8. $5\overline{)2145}$

9. Negative numbers are less than 0.   Circle: True   or   False

10. Write $\frac{7}{14}$ in its lowest terms. ....

My score: $\dfrac{}{10}$ **My time:** ....
                                                              minutes   seconds

Minute 73

Name: .... **Date:** ....

1. 14.018
   + 0.009

   ....

2. Zero is neither a positive number nor a negative number.

   Circle: True   or   False

3. $3\frac{3}{8} - 1\frac{1}{8} = \boxed{}\,\frac{\boxed{}}{8}$

4. Write the ratio of triangles to circles. .... : ....

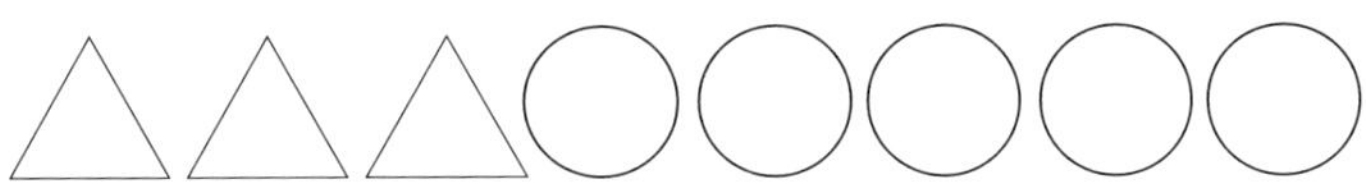

5. Write 0.09 as a percentage. ....%

6. $3\overline{)6.42}$ = ...

7. Write the decimal for 7%. ....

8. Write $\frac{3}{21}$ in its lowest terms. ....

9. Circle the name of the solid shape.

   square prism   triangular pyramid   triangular prism

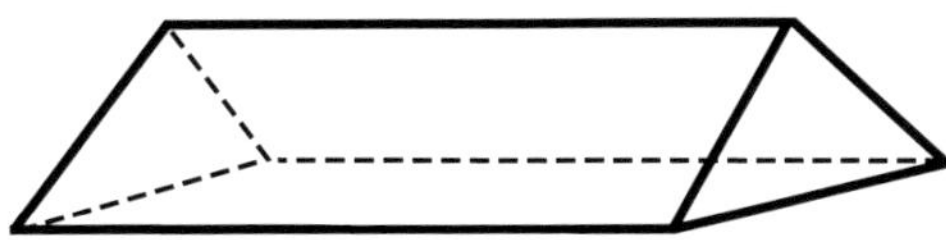

10. (1 m = 100 cm) 3.2 m = ... cm

My score: $\frac{}{10}$ **My time:** ....
                                                 minutes   seconds

Minute 74

Name: .... **Date:** ....

1. 10 x 0.06 = ...

2. Write $3\frac{5}{6}$ as an improper fraction. $\frac{\square}{6}$

Use the solid shape to complete Questions 3 and 4.

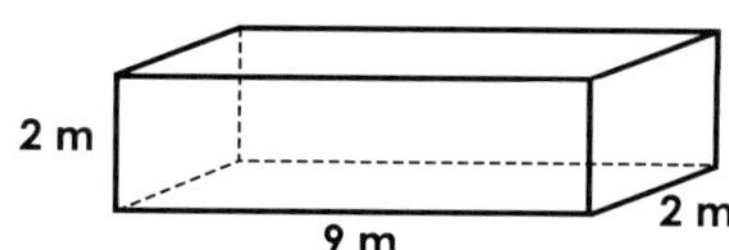

3. The solid has .... faces.

4. What is the volume of the solid? .... metres cubed $(v = l \times w \times h)$

5. $\frac{1}{3}\left(\frac{\square}{6}\right) + \frac{5}{6} = \frac{\square}{\square}$

6. $\frac{60}{100}$ = 0.60 = sixty hundredths   Circle: True   or   False

7. What is the highest common factor of 18 and 24?
    Circle the answer.

    3   6   12

8. $\frac{2}{3}$ of 9 = ...

9.   18.008
     +   5.716
     ....

     ....

10. What is the lowest common multiple of 4 and 6? ....

multiples	
4	6
4	6
8	12
12	18
16	24

My score: $\frac{\quad}{10}$ **My time:** ....
                  minutes   seconds

Minute 75

Name: .... **Date:** ....

1. Use <, > or =. $\frac{1}{2}$ .... $\frac{5}{10}$

2. 1901
       $\times$ 9
       ....

       ....

3. What is the lowest common multiple of 5 and 15? ....

Use the solid shape to complete Questions 4 and 5.

4. How many edges does the solid have? .... edges

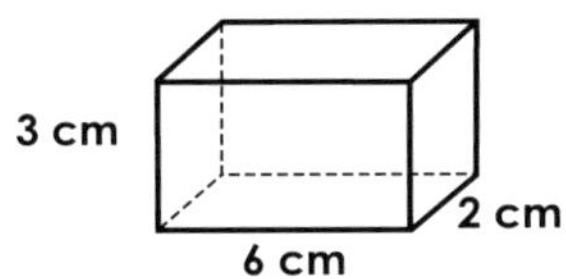

5. What is the volume of the solid? .... centimetres cubed (cm^3) ($v = l \times w \times h$)

6.   13.110
       + 6.418
       ....

       ....

7. $\frac{3}{5} - \frac{1}{5} =$ ....

8. $92 - x = 83$;

   therefore, $x =$ ....

9. What is the area of the triangle? .... square metres (m^2)

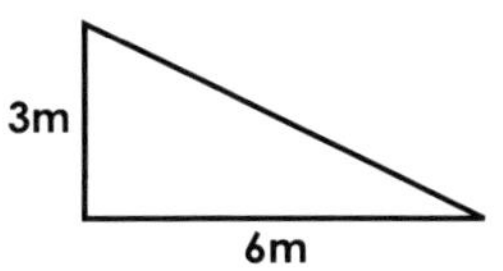

$$Area = \tfrac{1}{2} \times base \times height$$

10. Write the ratio of the number of school days in a week to the number

   of days in a weekend. .... : ....

My score: $\dfrac{\quad\quad}{10}$ **My time:** ....

                                            minutes   seconds

Minute 76

Name: .... **Date:** ....

1. $\begin{array}{r} 9.4 \\ \times\ \ 3 \\ \hline \\ \end{array}$

2. $39 \div 12 =$ .... r ....

3. Write a ratio of the number of months with the letter 'y' in the name to the number of months without the letter 'y' in the name.

   .... : ....

4. What is the area of the triangle? .... square metres (m^2)

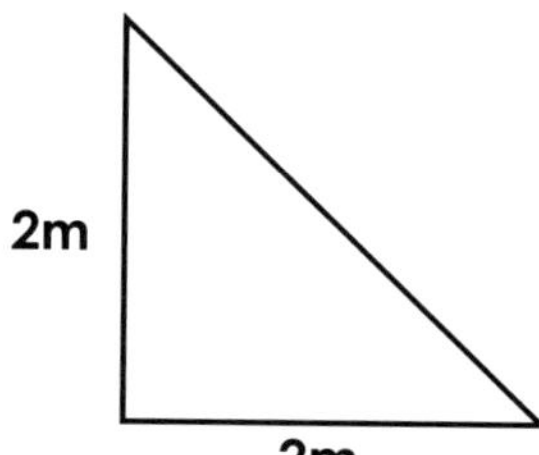

$Area = \frac{1}{2} \times base \times height$

5. $5\frac{1}{2} + 1\frac{1}{2} =$ ....

6. The lowest common multiple of 5 and 7 is ....

7. Circle the fraction equivalent to $\frac{3}{5}$. $\frac{6}{12}$ $\frac{9}{18}$ $\frac{12}{20}$

8. What is the volume of the solid? ....cubic metres (m^3)

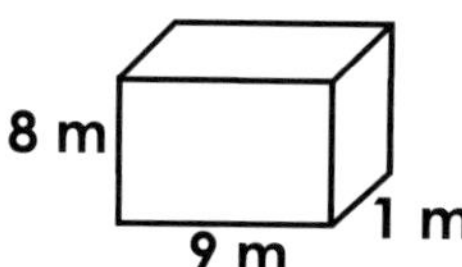

9. Write 5% as a decimal. ....

10. Circle the digit in the tenths place.   9.014

My score: $\dfrac{}{10}$

My time: ....
 minutes   seconds

Maths minutes

www.prim-ed.com   Prim-Ed Publishing®

Minute 77

Name: .... **Date:** ....

1. Write the numbers in order from highest to lowest.

   0.06   0.16   0.6   1.16

   ....

2. $\frac{7}{9} - \frac{5}{9} =$ ....

3. 17.12 + 3.70 = ...

4. Are the angles congruent? ....

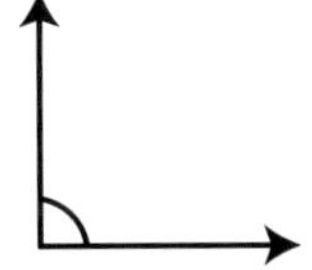
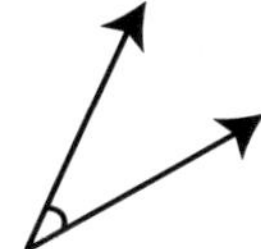

5. Write $\frac{9}{27}$ in its lowest terms. ....

6. $9\overline{)0.0144}$

7. $\frac{1}{5}$ of 10 = ...

8. What is the highest common factor of 2 and 10? ....

9. Write the ratio **3 to 5** as a fraction. ....

10. What is the area of the rectangle? .... square centimetres (cm^2)

   2 cm

   12 cm

My score: ___
10

My time: ....
minutes   seconds

Minute 78

Name: .... **Date:** ....

1. π is equal to about 3.14.   Circle: True   or   False

2. Is −5 a negative number? ....

3. Round 0.00**19** to the bold place. ....

4. Are the triangles congruent? ....

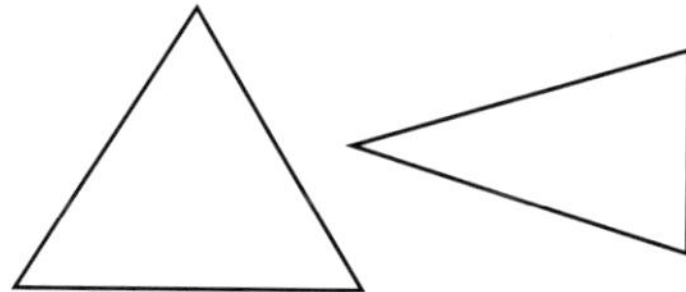

5. What is the lowest common multiple of 9 and 15? ....

6. $\frac{1}{2} + \frac{3}{4} = \frac{5}{4} = \boxed{} \frac{\boxed{}}{4}$

7. Write $5\frac{1}{8}$ as an improper fraction. $\frac{\boxed{}}{8}$

8. What is the area of the rectangle? .... mm^2

3 mm $\boxed{}$
6 mm

9. The simplest form of $\frac{12}{18}$ is ....

10. $\frac{2}{3}$ of 15 = 10   Circle: True   or   False

My score: $\dfrac{}{10}$ **My time:** ....
minutes   seconds

Minute 79

Name: .... **Date:** ....

1. Circle the digit in the thousandths place.   0.4815

2. Circle the fraction equivalent to $\frac{7}{9}$. $\frac{14}{20}$ $\frac{21}{27}$ $\frac{28}{45}$

3. Underline the circumference of the circle.   1.256   12.56   125.6

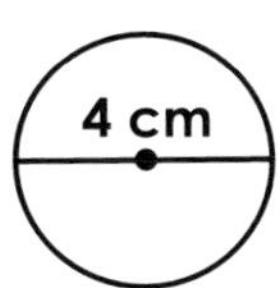

$Circumference \approx 3.14\ (\pi) \times diameter\ (d)$

$\approx 3.14 \times 4$

4. The simplest form of $\frac{9}{18}$ is ....

5.   852
    x   7
    ....

    ....

6. What is the lowest common factor of 9 and 14? ....

7. $\frac{4}{16} + \frac{5}{16} =$ ....

8. 0.12 ÷ 10 = ...

Use the solid shape to complete Questions 9 and 10.

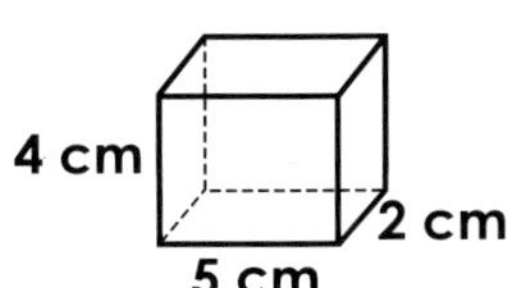

9. What is the volume of the solid? .... cm^3 $(v = l \times w \times h)$

10. The solid has .... faces.

My score: $\frac{\quad\quad}{10}$ **My time:** ....
                                                          minutes   seconds

Minute 80

Name: .... **Date:** ....

1. Write the fraction for 30%. ....

2. What is the area of the triangle? .... km²

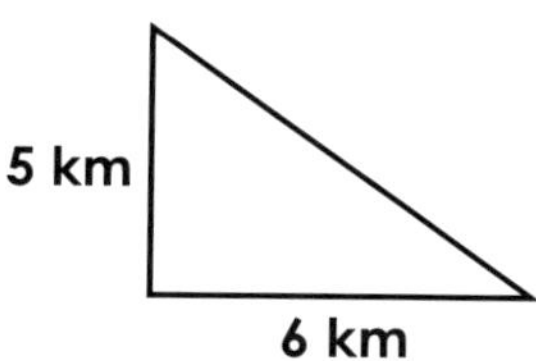

$A = \frac{1}{2} \times b \times h$ 　　　 $Area = \frac{1}{2} \times base \times height$

3. Write 0.65 as a percentage. ....%

4. $12\frac{3}{4} - 5\frac{1}{4} = \boxed{}\dfrac{\boxed{}}{4}$

5. Circle the digit in the hundredths place.   0.8912

6. Underline the circumference of the circle.   9.42   94.2   942

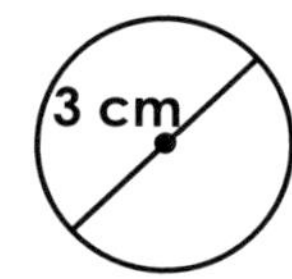

   circumference ≈ 3.14 (π) x diameter (d)

   　　　　　 ≈ 3.14 x 3

7. $\frac{1}{4}$ of 16 = ...

8.   1901
    x   9
    ....

    ....

9. 2000 g = ... kg

10. Use <, > or =. $\dfrac{5}{8}$ $\boxed{}$ $\dfrac{1}{4}$

My score: ______
10

My time: ....
　　　　　　　 minutes　　　　　　 seconds

Maths minutes

www.prim-ed.com　　Prim-Ed Publishing®

Minute 81

Name: .... **Date:** ....

1. $\frac{5}{9} + \frac{3}{9} =$ ....

2. Other than 1, what is the lowest common factor of 15 and 33? ....

3. Are the triangles congruent? ....

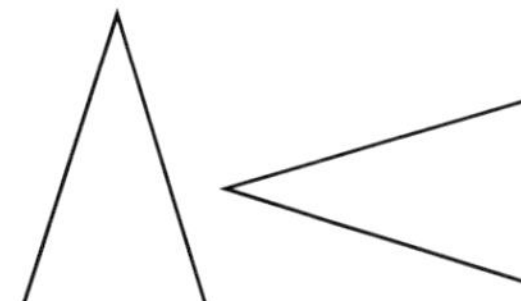

4. $\frac{1}{2}$ of 18 = ...

5. A mixed number is made up of a whole number and a fraction.

   Circle: True or False

6. Write 0.27 as a percentage. ....%

7. Write $\frac{18}{24}$ in its lowest terms. ....

Use the grid to complete Questions 8 to 10.

8. Name the point found at (3, 2). ....

9. What are the coordinates for point A? (..............)

10. Name the point found at (3, 4). ....

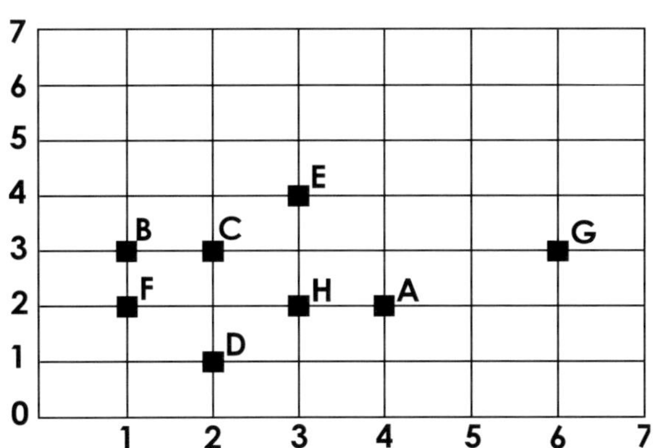

My score: $\frac{}{10}$

My time: ....
   minutes   seconds

Minute 82

Name: .... **Date:** ....

1. Write the numbers in order from lowest to highest.

    17.19   19.17   19.71   17.91

    ....

2. $4\frac{2}{9} + 2\frac{2}{9} =$ ....

3. $80 \times 70 =$ ....

4. A pair of numbers used to locate a point on a grid is called an ordered pair.

    Circle: True   or   False

5. What is 10% of 50? ....

6. $18 \times \frac{1}{2} =$ ....

7. 1000 m = ... km

8. Are the shapes congruent? ....

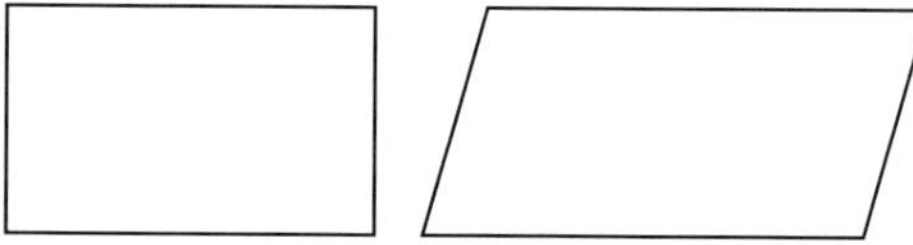

9.   8.5
    $\times$ 9
    ....

    ....

10. Circle the fraction equivalent to $\frac{7}{8}$. $\frac{14}{16}$ $\frac{20}{24}$ $\frac{21}{32}$

My score: $\frac{}{10}$ **My time:** ....

                                                                    minutes   seconds

Minute 83

Name: .... **Date:** ....

1. Use <, > or =.   112 + 8 .... 110 + 9

2. $\frac{5}{6} - \frac{1}{6} =$ ....

3. $\begin{array}{r} 411 \\ \times\ \ \ 9 \\ \hline \end{array}$

4. **Six metres below sea level** is a negative number.   Circle: True   or   False

5. 5 weeks = ... days

6. Use <, > or =.   4.440 .... 4.444

Use the grid to complete Questions 7 to 9.

7. Name the point found at (2, 3). ....

8. What are the coordinates for point E? (.............)

9. Name the point found at (5, 3). ....

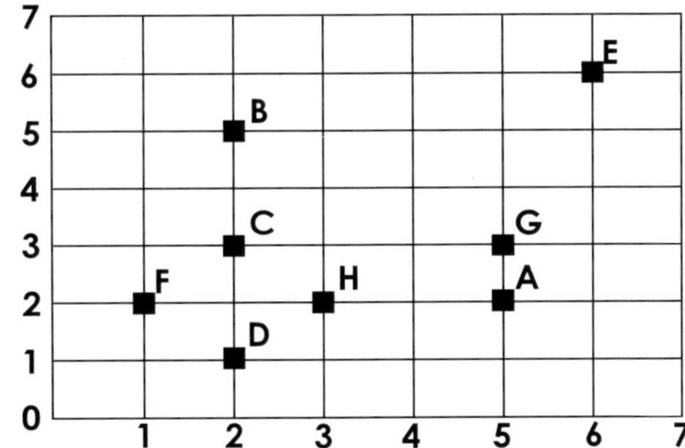

10. Use <, > or =. $\frac{2}{7}$ .... $\frac{3}{4}$

Minute 84

Name: .... **Date:** ....

1. 70 x 70 = ...

2. $\frac{4}{6} + \frac{1}{6}$ = ...

3. Are the shapes congruent? .... 

4. (2 x £1) + (5 x 5p) = £..............

5. Write the decimal for fifty-two hundredths. ....

6. 2000 mL = ... L   (1000 mL = 1 L)

7. Write $\frac{7}{100}$ as a percentage. ....%

8. What is the area of the triangle? .... cm^2

   (area = $\frac{1}{2}$ x base x height)

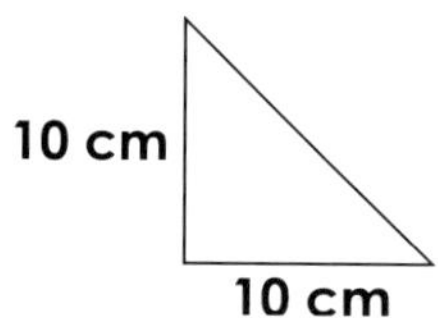

9.   1.9
   x   7
   ....

   ....

10. Write $7\frac{3}{4}$ as an improper fraction. ....

My score: $\frac{}{10}$ **My time:** ....
                                                              minutes   seconds

 Maths minutes

www.prim-ed.com   Prim-Ed Publishing®

Name: .... **Date:** ....

1. $8\frac{1}{2} - 6 =$ ....

2. Round **7**.11 to the bold place. ....

3. What is the area of the rectangle? .... km²

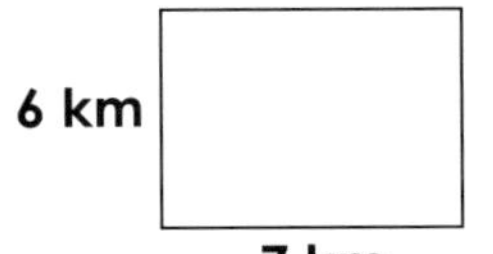

4. How long is the diameter of the circle? .... cm

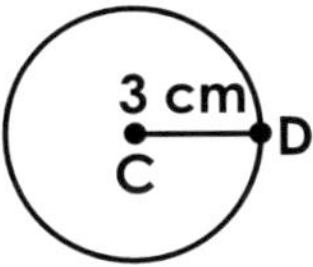

5. Use <, > or =. $\frac{3}{5}$ .... $\frac{5}{6}$

6. $7^2 = 7 \times 7 =$ ....

7. 12 km = ... m   (1 km = 1000 m)

8. Are the triangles congruent? ....

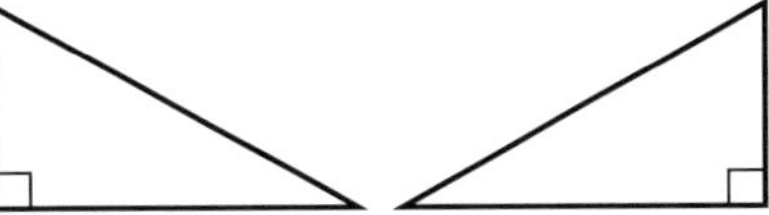

9. $4\overline{)12.84}$

10. Write the ratio **7 to 8** as a fraction. ....

My score: $\dfrac{\qquad}{10}$ **My time:** .... minutes .... seconds

Minute 86

Name: .... **Date:** ....

1. $10 \frac{5}{8} + 6 =$ ....

2. $\frac{1}{7}$ of 49 = ...

3. 11 mm = ... cm   (1 mm = 10 cm)

Use the grid to complete Questions 4 to 6.

4. Name the point found at (4, 3). ....

5. What are the coordinates for point F?

    (..............)

6. Name the point found at (2, 3). ....

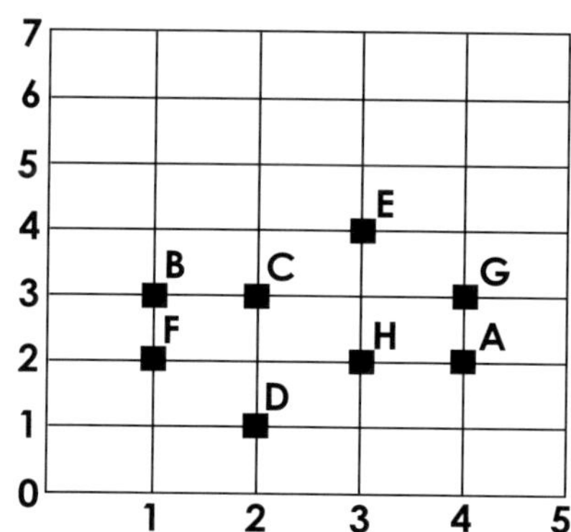

7. Circle the fraction equivalent to $\frac{1}{4}$. $\frac{2}{4}$ $\frac{3}{14}$ $\frac{4}{16}$

8. What is 68% of 100? ....

9. What is the lowest common multiple of 2 and 6? ....

10. What is the area of the triangle? .... cm^2 ($A = \frac{1}{2} \times b \times h$)

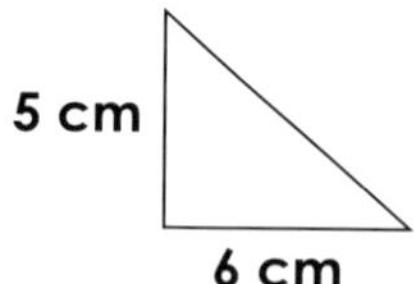

My score: $\frac{}{10}$ **My time:** ....

minutes   seconds

Minute 87

Name: .... **Date:** ....

1. 40 x 80 = ...

2. Write $\frac{16}{7}$ as a mixed number. ....

3. What is the area of the triangle? .... m^2

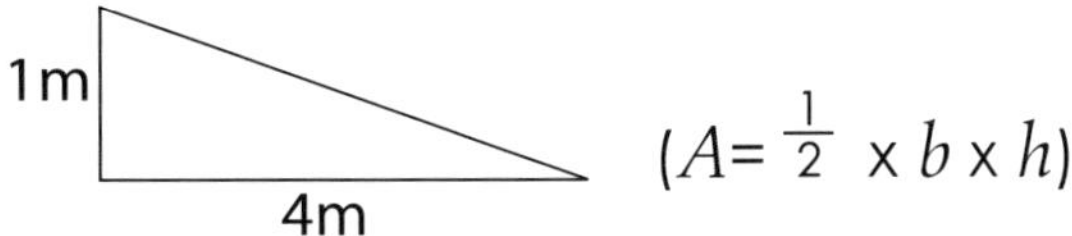

$(A = \frac{1}{2} \times b \times h)$

4. $\frac{1}{6}$ of 36 = ...

5. 16.4 ÷ 100 = ...

6. Write $\frac{1}{5}$ as a percentage. ....%

7. What is the volume of the cube? .... m^3

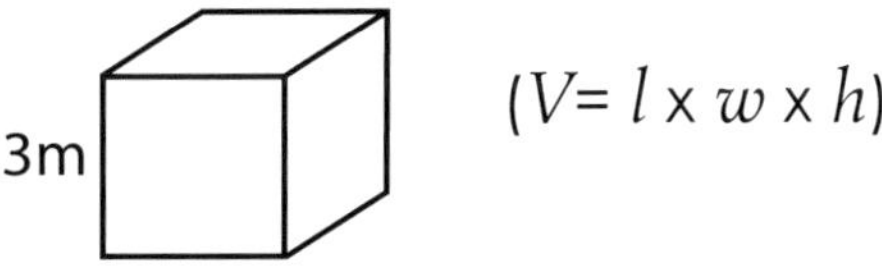

$(V = l \times w \times h)$

8. Circle the digit in the tenths place: 0.18

9. $\frac{1}{2} + \frac{1}{6}$ $\frac{1}{2}\left(\frac{\square}{6}\right) + \frac{1}{6} = \frac{\square}{6}$

10. What is the highest common factor of 16 and 20? ....

My score: $\frac{}{10}$ **My time:** ....
                                             minutes   seconds

Minute 88

Name: .... **Date:** ....

1. Use <, > or =.   657 921 .... 657 921

2. What is the area of the rectangle? .... mm²

$$6 \text{ mm} \quad \boxed{} \qquad a = l \times w$$

$$7 \text{ mm}$$

3. $\frac{5}{8} - \frac{1}{4} = \frac{5}{8} - \frac{1}{4} \left(\frac{\square}{8} \right) = \frac{\square}{8}$

4. Write 26% as a decimal. ....

5.
$$\begin{array}{r} 6 \\ 5 \\ 9 \\ 4 \\ + \ 1 \\ \hline \\ \hline \end{array}$$

6. Write $\frac{24}{64}$ in its lowest terms. ....

7. Are the triangles congruent? .... 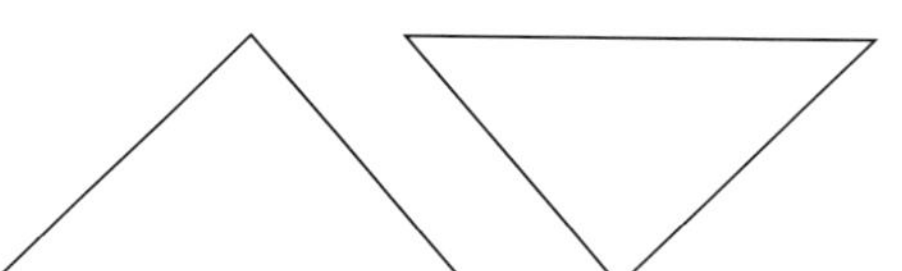

8. $\frac{1}{5}$ of 25 = ...

9. **Forty degrees above zero** is an example of a positive number.

   Circle: True or False

10. 1100 m = ... km

My score: $\frac{}{10}$

My time: ....
minutes   seconds

Minute 89

Name: .... **Date:** ....

1. 11 075
    −   859
    ....

    ....

2. Write $\frac{25}{40}$ in lowest terms. ....

3. $\frac{1}{7}$ of 14 = ...

4. $8\overline{)0.08}$

Use the grid to complete Questions 5 to 7.

5. Name the point at the coordinates (5, 1). ....

6. What are the coordinates for point C? (..............)

7. Name the point
   at the coordinates (6, 3). ....

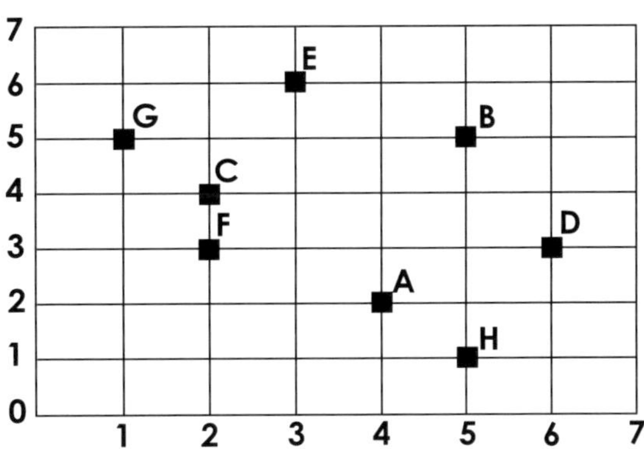

8. $\frac{2}{3} + \frac{5}{3} =$ ....

9. What is the lowest common multiple of 10 and 15? ....

10. Are the triangles congruent? ....

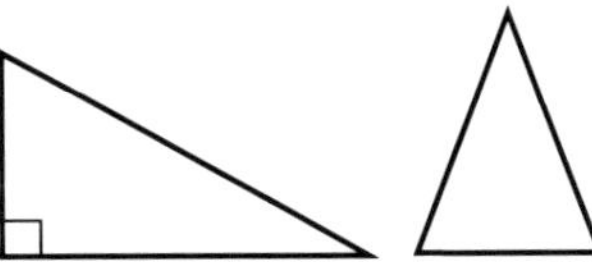

My score: $\frac{}{10}$

My time: ....
                    minutes   seconds

Minute 90

Name: .... **Date:** ....

1. $3 \div \frac{1}{2} = 3 \times \frac{2}{1}$ Circle: True or False

2. $0.8 \times 10 =$ ....

3. $\frac{2}{3} + \frac{2}{9} = \frac{2}{3} \left(\frac{\square}{9} \right) + \frac{2}{9} = \frac{\square}{9}$

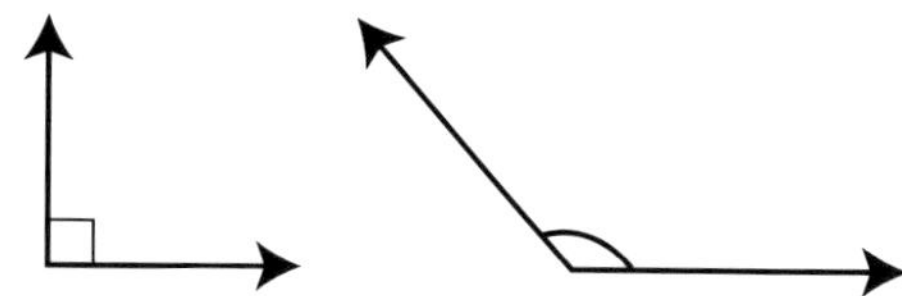

4. Circle the digit in the thousandths place. 19.3742

5. Are the angles congruent? ....

6. Circle the largest number.

   5 491 687   1 756 498   2 804 962

7. Write $\frac{10}{15}$ in lowest terms. ....

8. Write $\frac{9}{5}$ as a mixed number. ....

9. What is the area of the rectangle? .... cm^2 $(a = l \times w)$

   5 cm ▢ 7 cm

10. 3000 m = ... km

My score: $\dfrac{}{10}$ **My time:** ....
minutes   seconds

Minute 91

Name: .... **Date:** ....

1. $8\frac{1}{4} + 3 =$ ....

2. $5\overline{)20.90}$

Use the solid shape to complete Questions 3 and 4.

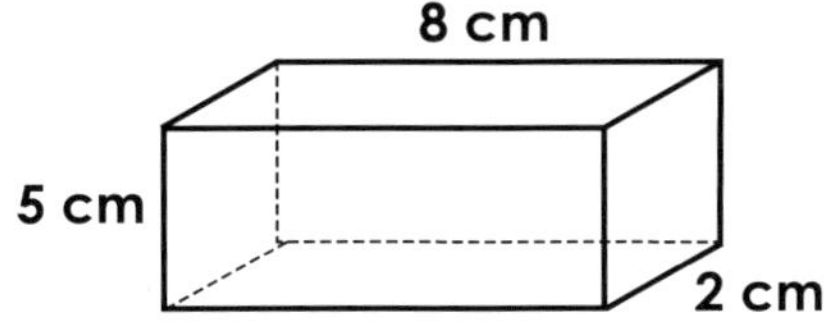

3. What is the volume of the solid? .... cm^3 ($v = l \times w \times h$)

4. The solid has .... edges.

5. Other than 1, what is the lowest common factor of 7 and 21? ....

6. Use <, > or =. $2\frac{2}{3}$ .... $3\frac{1}{4}$

7. 13 mm = ... cm

8. Write the ratio **11 to 20** as a fraction. ....

9. $\frac{1}{10}$ of 80 = ...

10. Complete the fact family.

    9 + 6 = 15   15 − 9 = 6

    ....

Minute 92

Name: .... **Date:** ....

1. Write 0.51 as a percentage. ....%

2. $10\frac{5}{7} - 8\frac{2}{7} =$ ....

3. Complete the fact family.

   $7 + 8 = 15$ $15 - 8 = 7$

   ....

4. 0.07 kg = ...g   (1 kg = 1000 g)

5. Are the triangles similar or congruent? ....

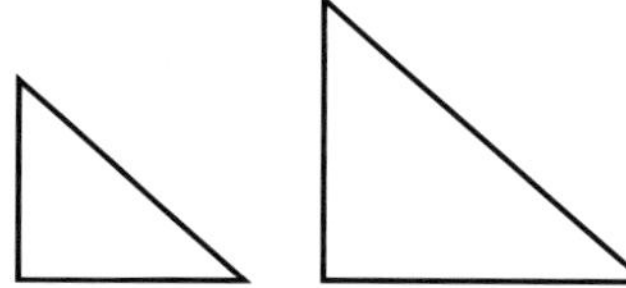

6. What is the lowest common multiple of 8 and 16? ....

7.   13.016
    x   2
    ....

    ....

8. Write the number: two million, seven hundred thousand,

   five hundred and sixty-three = ...

9. Write $\frac{11}{5}$ as a mixed number. ....

10. Circle the fraction equivalent to $\frac{2}{3}$. $\frac{4}{6}$ $\frac{6}{7}$ $\frac{5}{7}$

My score: $\frac{\qquad}{10}$ **My time:** ....
                                                     minutes   seconds

 Maths minutes

Minute 93

Name: .... **Date:** ....

1. $19.0 \div 1000 =$ ....

2. Other than 1, what is the lowest common factor of 12 and 20? ....

3. Are the triangles congruent or similar? ....

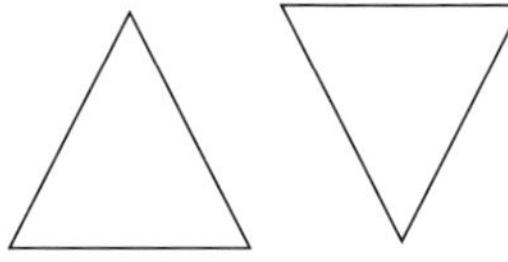

4. 86 301
   − 9 851
   ....

   ....

5. $\frac{3}{4}$ of 8 = ...

6. Use <, > or =. $5\frac{1}{7}$ .... $4\frac{3}{4}$

7. What is the area of the rectangle? .... mm^2

   3 mm ▭ 8 mm $(a = l \times w)$

8. $\frac{1}{9}$ of 81 = ...

9. Double 750. ....

10. $6\frac{2}{3} - 3\frac{1}{3} =$ ....

My score: $\dfrac{}{10}$

My time: ....
minutes   seconds

Minute 94

Name: .... **Date:** ....

1. Write $\frac{19}{4}$ as a mixed number. ....

2. Double 136. ....

3. 0.013 L = ... mL   (1L = 1000 mL)

4. $\frac{1}{8}$ of 24 = ...

5. Write $\frac{1}{4}$ as a percentage. ....%

6. Are the shapes similar? ....

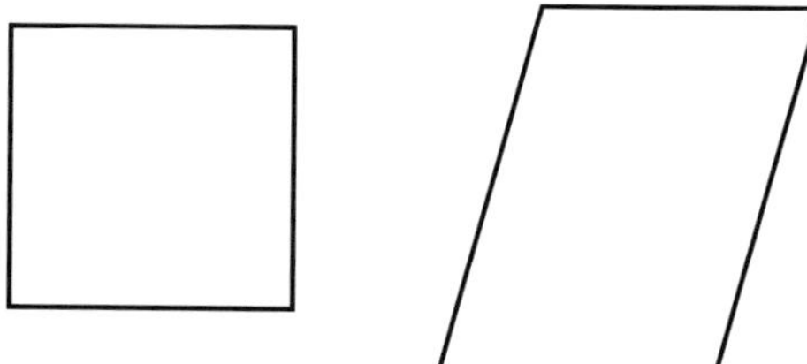

7. Write the numbers in order from highest to lowest.

   0.12   0.02   0.21   0.01

   ....

8. $\frac{5}{6} + \frac{1}{12}$ $\frac{5}{6} \left(\frac{\square}{12}\right) + \frac{1}{12} = \frac{\square}{12}$

9. Circle the digit in the hundredths place.   0.614

10. What is the area of the triangle? .... m² $\left(A = \frac{1}{2} \times b \times h\right)$

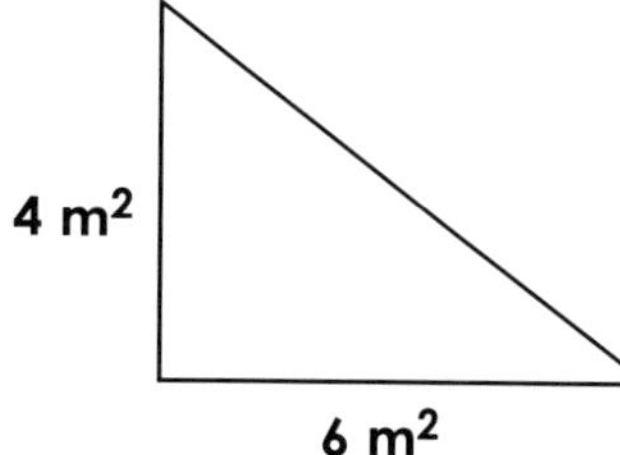

My score: $\frac{\quad}{10}$ **My time:** ....

minutes   seconds

Minute 95

Name: .... **Date:** ....

1. Write $\frac{40}{50}$ in lowest terms. ....

2. What is the area of the rectangle? .... m^2

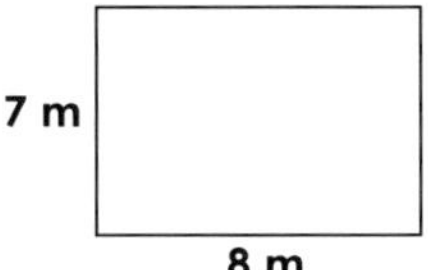

3. $31.4 \div 10 =$ ....

4. $\frac{3}{4} - \frac{1}{2}$ $\qquad$ $\frac{3}{4} - \frac{1}{2}$ $(\frac{}{4}) =$

5. Write the number in standard form: two million, four hundred and eleven thousand, three hundred and thirty-two.

   ....

6. Round to the bold place. 14.**4**6 ....

7. Are the angles congruent? ....

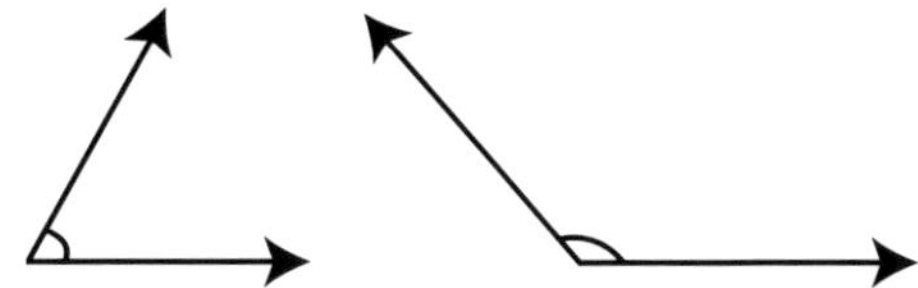

8. What is the lowest common multiple of 2 and 5? ....

9. Double 79 = ...

10. Write the ratio **15 to 32** as a fraction. ....

My score: $\dfrac{}{10}$

My time: ....

minutes $\qquad$ seconds

Minute 96

Name: .... **Date:** ....

1. $\frac{3}{8} + \frac{1}{8} =$ ....

2. Write 0.03 as a percentage. ....%

3. Circle the fraction equivalent to $\frac{5}{8}$. $\quad \frac{10}{12} \quad \frac{15}{24} \quad \frac{20}{36}$

4. $\quad 628$
   $-\ \ 47$
   ....

   ....

5. $\frac{2}{4}$ of 10 = ...

Use the grid to complete Questions 6 to 8.

6. Name the point at the coordinates (3, 4). ....

7. What are the coordinates for point B? (..............)

8. Name the point at the coordinates (4, 1). ....

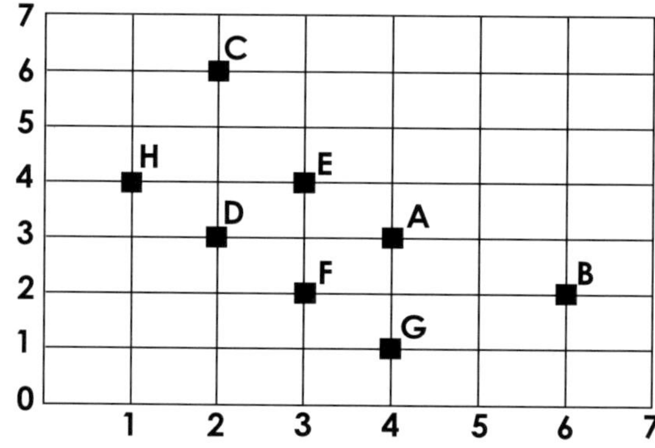

9. Circle the digit in the tenths place. $\qquad$ 193.08

10. Name the solid shape. .... prism.

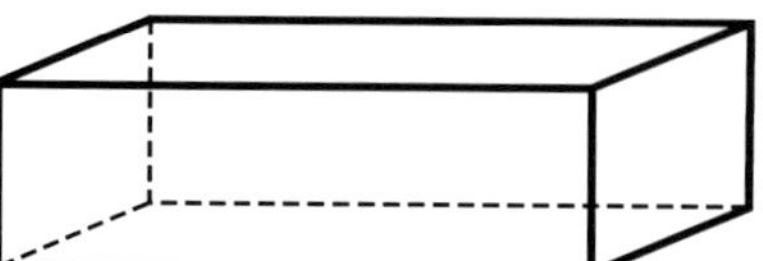

My score: $\frac{\quad\quad}{10}$

My time: ....
$\qquad$ minutes $\qquad\qquad$ seconds

Maths minutes

www.prim-ed.com $\quad$ Prim-Ed Publishing®

Minute 97

Name: .... **Date:** ....

1. Circle the fraction equivalent to $\frac{5}{6}$. $\frac{15}{12}$ $\frac{12}{18}$ $\frac{30}{36}$

2. Use <, > or =.   5 256 734 .... 5 256 734

3. Are the shapes similar or congruent? ....

4. $2\overline{)18.86}$

5. Write 17% as a fraction. ....

6.   148 565
        $-$ 15 178
        ....

        ....

7. $\frac{1}{2} + \frac{3}{8}$ 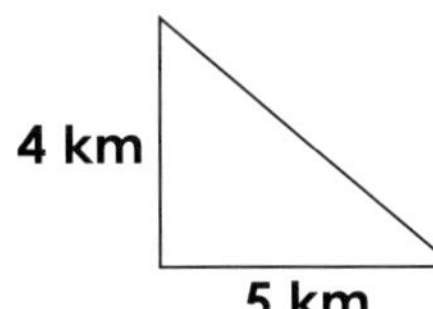

8. 10 mm = ... cm

9. What is the area of the triangle? .... km^2

4 km
5 km
$(A = \frac{1}{2} \times b \times h)$

10. $\frac{4}{4}$ of 12 = ...

My score: $\frac{\quad\quad}{10}$ **My time:** .... minutes .... seconds

Minute 98

Name: .... **Date:** ....

1. Write $\frac{6}{9}$ in lowest terms. ....

2.   12.7
     x   5
       ....

       ....

3. Write $\frac{9}{10}$ as a percentage. ....%

4. 176 m = ... km   (1 m = 1000 km)

5. $\frac{5}{6}$ of 12 = ...

Use the grid to complete Questions 6 to 8.

6. Name the point at the coordinates (2, 1). ....

7. What are the coordinates for point E? ....

8. Name the point at the coordinates (4, 5). ....

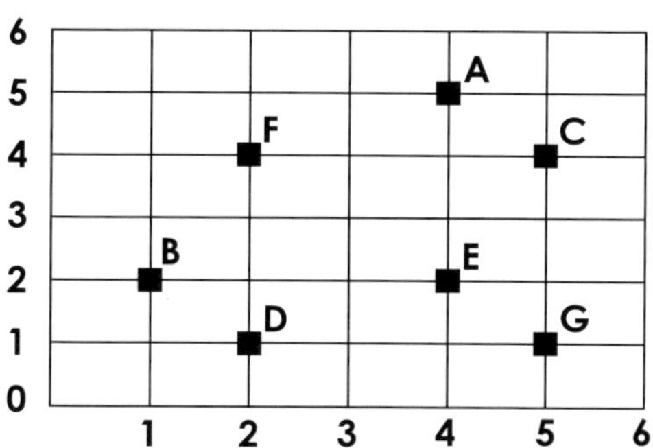

9. $\frac{1}{3} - \frac{1}{6}$ $\frac{1}{3} \left(\frac{\square}{6} \right) - \frac{\square}{6} = \frac{\square}{6}$

10. Are the angles congruent? ....

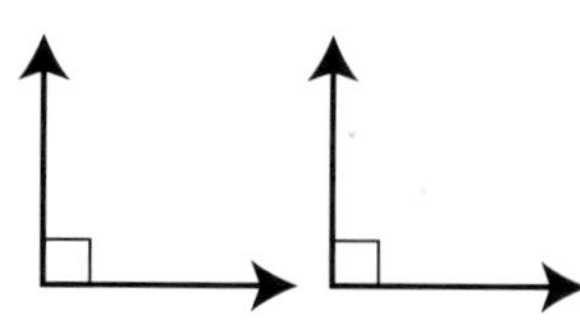

My score: $\frac{\qquad}{10}$ **My time:** ....
                                                          minutes   seconds

Minute 99

Name: .... **Date:** ....

1. $5\overline{)0.0075}$

2. $\frac{4}{9} - \frac{1}{9} =$ ....

3. What is the area of the rectangle? .... cm^2

2 cm | 4 cm (rectangle)

4.
```
     3
     4
     8
     7
 +   6
 ........
```

5. Circle the digit in the millions place.

   4 715 823

6. $2\frac{1}{3} + 5\frac{1}{3} =$ ....

7. What is the radius of the circle? .... cm

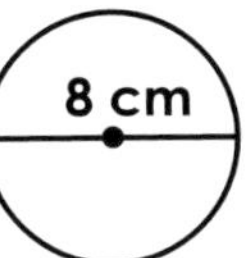

8. What is 50% of 500? ....

9. Are the triangles similar or congruent? ....

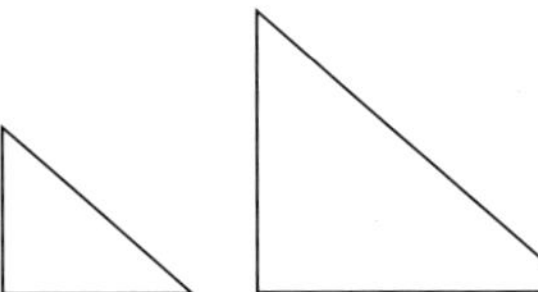

10. Write $\frac{11}{6}$ as a mixed number. ....

My score: $\frac{}{10}$

My time: ....
minutes   seconds

Minute 100

Name: .... **Date:** ....

1. Write the number in standard form:

   two hundred and two thousand, one hundred and sixty-two. ....

2. $\frac{3}{4}$ of £8.00 = £.............

Use the grid to complete Questions 3 to 5.

3. Name the point at the coordinates (4, 2). ....

4. What are the coordinates for point D? ....

5. Name the point at the coordinates (5, 2). ....

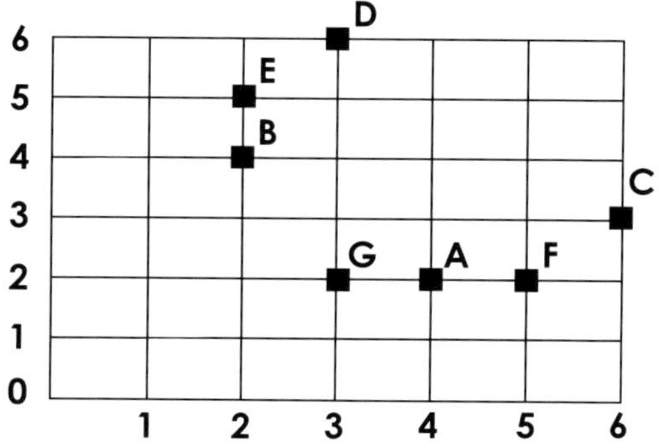

6. What percentage of 10 is 5? ....

7.   910
   + 813
   ....

   ....

8. 100 x 0.003 = ...

9. $4\frac{1}{2} - 2\frac{1}{2}$ = ...

10. Write the volume of the solid. .... cm³

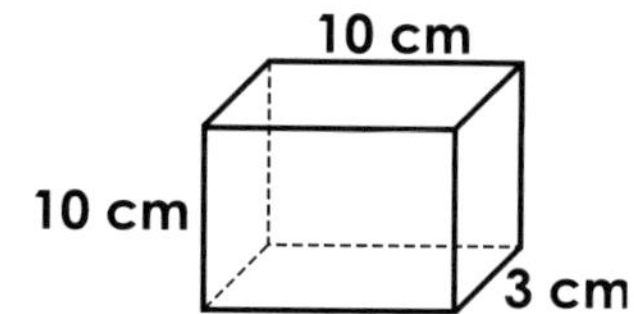

$V = l \times w \times h$

My score: $\frac{\quad\quad}{10}$

My time: ....
                minutes   seconds

Minute answer key

Minute 1
1. 7
2. 12
3. No
4. 10
5. 12.00 midnight
6. 32%
7. football, hockey
8. basketball
9. 4
10. 100

Minute 2
1. 25
2. 5
3. 15
4. 11
5. 5
6. 8 + 6 = 14
7. True
8. $\frac{1}{2}$
9. 60
10. 12, 15, 18

Minute 3
1. 473 665
2. 8
3. clean their room
4. go to cinema
5. play outside
6. 49
7. 5.00 pm
8. cone
9. 12 − 8 = 4
10. 140

Minute 4
1. 25
2. 40
3. 95
4. 6 x 7 = 42
5. 48
6. 10
7. 20
8. $\frac{2}{3}$
9. 48
10. Subtract 11

Minute 5
1. 5
2. 40
3. 18 000
4. No
5. 69
6. 646 354
7. $\frac{2}{5}$
8. 42, 32, 22
9. 20
10. 25

Minute 6
1. 21
2. 244
3. 6 + 7 = 13
4. 80
5. 7
6. 1000
7. True
8. 200
9. 13
10. square pyramid

Minute 7
1. 11 − 3 = 8
2. 299
3. 10
4. increase
5. 24
6. 10
7. 1500 m
8. 90, 80, 70
9. $\frac{3}{7}$
10. 200

Minute 8
1. 700
2. 421
3. 12 x 8 = 96
4. 56
5. True
6. 4.00 am
7. 8
8. octagon
9. 3000
10. 101 r 1

Minute 9
1. 0
2. 86
3. 157
4. PE
5. 60
6. 9
7. 1000
8. $\frac{6}{9}$ or $\frac{2}{3}$
9. $1\frac{1}{2}$ or 1.5
10. 6

Minute 10
1. 7 hundred
2. 1000
3. 36
4. Yes
5. $\frac{3}{8}$
6. 150
7. 7 x 11 = 77
8. 17
9. 4
10. 150

Minute 11
1. 831 894
2. 50
3. 908
4. Yes
5. 6
6. 150
7. 21
8. 86 − 42 = 44
9. line
10. 15 000

Minute 12
1. 544
2. 32, 36, 40
3. 14
4. 680 mm
5. 933 085
6. 7.00 pm
7. 28 ÷ 7 = 4
8. Dance
9. Drama
10. cube

Minute 13
1. millions
2. 20
3. 10
4. <
5. 36
6. Yes
7. 3000
8. 8610
9. $\frac{3}{4}$
10. 1 r 3

Minute 14
1. 28
2. 18
3. 535
4. composite number
5. 15
6. 2.5
7. 7, 9, 11
8. 10
9. forty-two thousand, two hundred and thirty-four
10. cylinder

Minute 15
1. 7000
2. 9
3. 10
4. 8991
5. 1000
6. <
7. 19
8. sphere
9. 32, 64, 128
10. 1400

Minute 16
1. >
2. 94 400
3. 70
4. True
5. 42, 49, 56
6. 8 x 3 = 24
7. 80
8. 5
9. 3
10. parallelogram

Minute 17
1. 12 811
2. 15 − 6 = 9
3. 3
4. 180
5. 99
6. 2 r 4
7. £5.85
8. $\frac{5}{6}$
9. 2000
10. 1.8

Minute 18
1. 637 151
2. 46
3. 1
4. 1200
5. 3
6. 80
7. 10
8. False
9. grapes
10. bananas

Minute 19
1. 8
2. 29
3. 20
4. 42
5. £2.50
6. 3
7. 900
8. 0
9. $2\frac{1}{2}$ or 2.5
10. trapezium

Minute 20
1. >
2. 180
3. 6
4. 48, 40, 32
5. 372 512
6. 30°
7. 8
8. 180
9. dog
10. 40%

Minute answer key

Minute 21
1. 35
2. 335
3. 111 636
4. 16
5. 70
6. 9 r 3
7. 65 000
8. 233, 244
9. 392, 923, 3092, 3920
10. ○, □, ○

Minute 22
1. 40
2. 24 r 1
3. 102 + 60 = 162
4. 43 190
5. No
6. Quiz 4
7. improve
8. <
9. 4
10. 20

Minute 23
1. 11.6
2. 6 030 070
3. 16
4. 127
5. 5 − 3 = 2
6. £15.00
7. 40°
8. 3 000 000
9. 12
10. £7.96

Minute 24
1. 8.05, 8.40, 8.45, 8.54
2. 96
3. 16.151
4. 110
5. 2949
6. 14
7. 60 thousands
8. 24 ÷ 3 = 8
9. £1.41
10. ▽

Minute 25
1. 39 279
2. 1523
3. 120
4. 71 000
5. 243
6. 11
7. 4
8. 22%
9. 6
10. 19.42, 19.24, 14.92, 14.29

Minute 26
1. 425
2. 4
3. 6 + 5 = 11
4. 450
5. 30 °C
6. True
7. <
8. 6 r 2
9. 15
10. No

Minute 27
1. 1541
2. 0.4
3. 140
4. £18.00
5. 2425
6. 54 ÷ 6 = 9
7. 19 000
8. prime number
9. 13
10. equilateral

Minute 28
1. 0
2. 90
3. £0.51
4. 35
5. 18
6. 14
7. False
8. 31
9. 1.30, 0.31, 0.13, 0.013
10. $\frac{3}{6}$ or $\frac{1}{2}$

Minute 29
1. 5 + 7 = 12
2. 3754
3. No
4. 40°
5. 23.23
6. 0
7. £29.50
8. £1.52
9. right-angle
10. 15

Minute 30
1. 100
2. 18
3. 50
4. 3.1
5. £13.58
6. 7
7. 4000
8. 13 − 8 = 5
9. yes
10. 15.16, 16.01, 16.15, 16.51

Minute 31
1. 851
2. 5
3. 1 070 409
4. 350
5. right
6. £3.00
7. 32 ÷ 4 = 8
8. 1443
9. 3
10. 7

Minute 32
1. 10
2. 180
3. Yes
4. 15
5. 9
6. 712
7. 24
8. 20
9. <
10. □, ⬠

Minute 33
1. 104 498
2. 4
3. winter
4. Favourite seasons
5. spring, summer
6. 32 ÷ 4 = 8
7. 16
8. 3000
9. 10.33, 10.30, 10.03, 1.03
10. 20p, 20p, 20p, 5p
   or
   50p, 10p, 5p

Minute 34
1. 6250
2. 4
3. 72
4. 0
5. 12.62
6. 4800
7. 11
8. £9.33
9. <
10. 16

Minute 35
1. 2.05
2. 442
3. 2
4. 12
5. □, ▯
6. 8
7. 4200
8. £53
9. 9.26
10. 0

Minute 36
1. 16.1
2. 102
3. Yes
4. 75
5. 1348
6. 15
7. 19
8. £7.28
9. isosceles
10. 16

Minute 37
1. 6 x 3 = 18
2. £1.66
3. 15°C
4. 6500
5. 10
6. 1
7. No
8. £8.88
9. 9
10. 3132

Minute 38
1. 14
2. 0.81, 0.18, 0.08, 0.01
3. 340
4. 20
5. 15
6. 13 000
7. 3, 30
8. 18
9. scalene
10. ⬠, □

Minute 39
1. 12
2. 558
3. 195.48
4. 0.045
5. 1
6. 1342
7. acute
8. stay after school
9. 150
10. parent pick-up

Minute 40
1. 1645
2. 1
3. 1330
4. 1
5. 192
6. 35.26
7. 4
8. 16
9. 3, 10
10. 32

Maths minutes

Minute answer key

Minute 41
1. £29.44
2. 0.21
3. 15
4. 28 m 20 cm
5. True
6. £2.96
7. 12
8. 270
9. 24
10. 1

Minute 42
1. 90
2. True
3. 12
4. £37.84
5. 3
6. 16.29
7. 125
8. 8
9. 12°
10. 120

Minute 43
1. 250
2. £0.91
3. True
4. 2
5. >
6. £60.25
7. 12 900
8. obtuse
9. 20
10. 4

Minute 44
1. £55.50
2. £21.00
3. 320
4. 56
5. 14
6. $\frac{1}{2}$
7. 240
8. obtuse
9. True
10. 17

Minute 45
1. yes
2. 3
3. False
4. A
5. 12
6. 2, 5
7. 2.5
8. 26
9. 3606
10. 340

Minute 46
1. £2.00
2. £5.68
3. 6.35
4. £28.10
5. 4 r 1
6. No
7. obtuse
8. 30 635
9. True
10. 180

Minute 47
1. 0.6
2. 3
3. £49.00
4. 24
5. 2, 33
6. hexagon
7. 170°
8. 16.99
9. 208
10. ○, ●

Minute 48
1. 11
2. 6
3. £0.52
4. True
5. £73.62
6. 7, 50
7. 39 °C
8. 0
9. £12.30
10. 103

Minute 49
1. 12%
2. 7.2
3. 7200mL
4. False
5. 4040mL
6. 2442
7. 1
8. 25°
9. $\overline{GH}$
10. 1848

Minute 50
1. £36.41
2. 18
3. rhombus
4. £12.70
5. 40 cm
6. 2, 6
7. 18 117
8. right
9. 2 r 6
10. △

Minute 51
1. £16.24
2. 0.2
3. 4000
4. 16 ÷ 8 = 2
5. 1624
6. 3, 36
7. Octagon
8. 90°
9. 12
10. True

Minute 52
1. £8.55
2. Yes
3. 0.072
4. 4200
5. 62
6. 26.23
7. 240
8. 18 682
9. yes
10. equilateral

Minute 53
1. 7
2. trapezium
3. £0.70
4. yes
5. 15
6. 168
7. 27 °C
8. 0.018
9. difference
10. quotient

Minute 54
1. 10
2. £32.84
3. 10.15
4. 32
5. 304
6. 1, 3
7. 1.62
8. acute
9. 6
10. True

Minute 55
1. 17.1
2. 200.9
3. 14%
4. 5
5. 109
6. yes
7. 32 880
8. sphere
9. equilateral
10. plane

Minute 56
1. 46%
2. 0.8
3. 21
4. $\overline{DC}$
5. plane
6. ray
7. point
8. 1, 30
9. ∠ ZYX
10. 1020

Minute 57
1. True
2. 90°
3. 0.705
4. 280
5. 15
6. 1.12
7. 36 108
8. 125°
9. True
10. perimeter

Minute 58
1. 5.08
2. £2.05
3. 267
4. no
5. 34.22
6. 1, 40
7. NML
8. True
9. 156
10. £0.95

Minute 59
1. £55.20
2. 4.02
3. 21
4. 140
5. 81
6. perpendicular
7. >
8. =
9. 0.2
10. True

Minute 60
1. 75%
2. $\frac{5}{10}$ or $\frac{1}{2}$
3. 2811
4. 15
5. 4, 46
6. 0.3
7. acute
8. mystery
9. 20
10. 15

Minute answer key

Minute 61
1. 1.8
2. £0.27
3. 70°
4. 0.64
5. 27
6. 3, 0
7. $1\frac{4}{6}$, $1\frac{2}{3}$
8. 20.604
9. 16
10. diameter

Minute 62
1. 9.6
2. £11.04
3. 7250
4. no
5. 2.01
6. 103
7. 3
8. $2\frac{5}{6}$
9. isosceles
10. 270

Minute 63
1. £35.07
2. 1.058
3. 2.05
4. 176
5. ellipse
6. 70
7. 45°
8. 748
9. $\frac{2}{4}$ or $\frac{1}{2}$
10. 3%

Minute 64
1. 8 r 1
2. >
3. 4.02
4. 300
5. 2
6. 0.02
7. scalene
8. $\frac{5}{7}$
9. 5
10. 20

Minute 65
1. 64%
2. 60
3. £12.15
4. 6500
5. no
6. 8750
7. 52
8. right-angle
9. $\frac{2}{8}$, $\frac{5}{8}$
10. 1, 20

Minute 66
1. £22.08
2. 6
3. 1.14
4. 35
5. $\frac{2}{7}$
6. 75%
7. £4.60
8. 0
9. 90
10. 198

Minute 67
1. £19.02
2. 14
3. 47%
4. $\frac{3}{5}$
5. yes
6. True
7. 2:4
8. sunny
9. April
10. Feb. and May

Minute 68
1. 3:5
2. $\overline{HJ}$
3. True
4. 6.5
5. 5.2
6. True
7. $5\frac{4}{5}$
8. 5
9. 28 mm
10. 6.81

Minute 69
1. 101
2. True
3. $\frac{6}{10}$ $\frac{9}{10}$
4. 7
5. 2.172
6. True
7. 2085
8. 2:3
9. False
10. 2

Minute 70
1. 50%
2. £1.76
3. $\frac{3}{6}$
4. 2
5. $3\frac{1}{3}$
6. 36.26
7. 10.596
8. □,□,□,□,O
9. 36
10. 6

Minute 71
1. 0
2. $6\frac{3}{8}$
3. 4:5
4. 3
5. 1510
6. 4.132
7. $\frac{11}{4}$
8. True
9. 5
10. $3\frac{1}{2}$

Minute 72
1. =
2. $\frac{5}{4}$ or $1\frac{1}{4}$
3. 10.75
4. 3
5. $\frac{12}{BA}$
6.
7. 20
8. 429
9. True
10. $\frac{1}{2}$

Minute 73
1. 14.027
2. True
3. $2\frac{2}{8}$ or $2\frac{1}{4}$
4. 3:5
5. 9%
6. 2.14
7. 0.07
8. $\frac{1}{7}$
9. triangular prism
10. 320

Minute 74
1. 0.6
2. $\frac{23}{6}$
3. 6
4. 36
5. $\frac{7}{6}$ or $1\frac{1}{6}$
6. True
7. 6
8. 6
9. 23.724
10. 12

Minute 75
1. =
2. 17 109
3. 15
4. 12
5. 36
6. 19.528
7. $\frac{2}{5}$
8. 9
9. 9
10. 5:2

Minute 76
1. 28.2
2. 3 r 3
3. 4:8
4. 2
5. 7
6. 35
7. $\frac{12}{20}$
8. 72
9. 0.05
10. 0

Minute 77
1. 1.16, 0.6, 0.16, 0.06
2. $\frac{2}{9}$
3. 20.82
4. no
5. $\frac{1}{3}$
6. 0.0016
7. 2
8. 2
9. $\frac{3}{5}$
10. 24

Minute 78
1. True
2. yes
3. 0.00
4. no
5. 45
6. $1\frac{1}{4}$
7. $\frac{41}{8}$
8. 18
9. $\frac{2}{3}$
10. True

Minute 79
1. 1
2. $\frac{21}{27}$
3. 12.56
4. $\frac{1}{2}$
5. 5964
6. 1
7. $\frac{9}{16}$
8. 0.012
9. 40
10. 6

Minute 80
1. $\frac{30}{100}$ or $\frac{3}{10}$
2. 15
3. 65%
4. $7\frac{2}{4}$ or $7\frac{1}{2}$
5. 9
6. 9.42
7. 4
8. 17 109
9. 2
10. >

Minute answer key

Minute 81
1. $\frac{8}{9}$
2. 3
3. yes
4. 9
5. True
6. 27%
7. $\frac{3}{4}$
8. H
9. (4, 2)
10. E

Minute 82
1. 17.19, 17.91, 19.17, 19.71
2. $6\frac{4}{9}$
3. 5600
4. True
5. 5
6. 9
7. 1
8. no
9. 76.5
10. $\frac{14}{16}$

Minute 83
1. >
2. $\frac{4}{6}$ or $\frac{2}{3}$
3. 3699
4. True
5. 35
6. <
7. C
8. (6, 6)
9. G
10. <

Minute 84
1. 4900
2. $\frac{5}{6}$
3. no
4. £2.25
5. 0.52
6. 2
7. 7%
8. 50
9. 13.3
10. $\frac{31}{4}$

Minute 85
1. $2\frac{1}{2}$
2. 7
3. 42
4. 6
5. <
6. 49
7. 12 000
8. yes
9. 3.21
10. $\frac{7}{8}$

Minute 86
1. $16\frac{5}{8}$
2. 7
3. 1.1
4. G
5. (1, 2)
6. C
7. $\frac{4}{16}$
8. 68
9. 6
10. 15

Minute 87
1. 3200
2. $2\frac{2}{7}$
3. 2
4. 6
5. 0.164
6. 20%
7. 27
8. 1
9. $\frac{4}{6}$ or $\frac{2}{3}$
10. 4

Minute 88
1. =
2. 42
3. $\frac{3}{8}$
4. 0.26
5. 25
6. $\frac{3}{8}$
7. yes
8. 5
9. True
10. 1.1

Minute 89
1. 10 216
2. $\frac{5}{8}$
3. 2
4. 0.01
5. H
6. (2, 4)
7. D
8. $\frac{7}{3}$ or $2\frac{1}{3}$
9. 30
10. no

Minute 90
1. True
2. 8
3. $\frac{8}{9}$
4. 4
5. no
6. 5 491 687
7. $\frac{2}{3}$
8. $1\frac{4}{5}$
9. 35
10. 3

Minute 91
1. $11\frac{1}{4}$
2. 4.18
3. 80
4. 12
5. 7
6. <
7. 1.3
8. $\frac{11}{20}$
9. 8
10. 6 + 9 = 15, 15 − 6 = 9

Minute 92
1. 51%
2. $2\frac{3}{7}$
3. 8 + 7 = 15, 15 − 7 = 8
4. 70
5. similar
6. 16
7. 26.032
8. 2 700 563
9. $2\frac{1}{5}$
10. $\frac{4}{6}$

Minute 93
1. 0.019
2. 2
3. congruent
4. 76 450
5. 6
6. >
7. 24
8. 9
9. 1500
10. $3\frac{1}{3}$

Minute 94
1. $4\frac{3}{4}$
2. 272
3. 13
4. 3
5. 25%
6. no
7. 0.21, 0.12, 0.02, 0.01
8. $\frac{10}{12}, \frac{11}{12}$
9. 1
10. 12

Minute 95
1. $\frac{4}{5}$
2. 56
3. 3.14
4. $\frac{1}{4}$
5. 2 411 332
6. 14.5
7. no
8. 10
9. 158
10. $\frac{15}{32}$

Minute 96
1. $\frac{4}{8}$ or $\frac{1}{2}$
2. 3%
3. $\frac{15}{24}$
4. 581
5. 5
6. E
7. (6, 2)
8. G
9. 0
10. rectangular prism

Minute 97
1. $\frac{30}{36}$
2. =
3. similar
4. 9.43
5. $\frac{17}{100}$
6. 133 387
7. $\frac{4}{8}, \frac{7}{8}$
8. 1
9. 10
10. 12

Minute 98
1. $\frac{2}{3}$
2. 63.5
3. 90%
4. 0.176
5. 10
6. D
7. (4, 2)
8. A
9. $\frac{1}{6}$
10. yes

Minute 99
1. 0.0015
2. $\frac{3}{9}$ or $\frac{1}{3}$
3. 8
4. 28
5. 4
6. $7\frac{2}{3}$
7. 4
8. 250
9. similar
10. $1\frac{5}{6}$

Minute 100
1. 202 162
2. £6.00
3. A
4. (3, 6)
5. F
6. 50%
7. 1723
8. 0.3
9. 2
10. 300